Women of the Golden State:

25 California Women You Should Know

© 2009 Apprentice Shop Books, LLC • Bedford, New Hampshire

Written by Linda Crotta Brennan and Others • Illustrated by Lisa Greenleaf

Apprentice Shop Books, LLC
Bedford, New Hampshire

For information regarding permissions contact:
Apprentice Shop Books, LLC
7 Colby Court, Box 156
Bedford, NH 03110
www.apprenticeshopbooks.com

LIBRARY OF CONGRESS CATALOGING-IN-PUBLICATION DATA

Brennan, Linda Crotta

Women of the Golden State: 25 California Women You Should Know by Linda Crotta Brennan, Deborah Bruss, Marty Darragh, Joyce Ray, and Others
Illustrations copyright © 2009 by Lisa Greenleaf

Summary: Profiles of 25 influential California women. Includes bibliographies for additional research.

1.California, Juvenile non-fiction. 2. Famous California women. 3. Women artists—United States—California—biography—juvenile literature. 4. Women athletes—United States—California—biography—juvenile literature. 5. Women writers—United States—California—biography—juvenile literature. 6. Women in public service—United States—California—juvenile literature.

ISBN-13: 978-0-9723410-6-6

Kase Printing
13 Hampshire Drive
Hudson, NH 03051

Printed in USA

On the cover: Clockwise from bottom right: Nancy Pelosi, Maxine Hong Kingston, Bridget "Biddy" Mason, Ruth Law, Dolores Huerta, Maud Younger and Betty Ford

 Cover design, illustrations, and book design by Lisa Greenleaf
Greenleaf Design Studio *www.Lisagreenleaf.com*

15 14 13 12 11 10 9 8 7 6 5 4 3 2 1

A Timeline of California History

1776 ► Spanish colonizers settle the Presidio and Mission Dolores in present-day San Francisco.

1821 ► Mexico wins independence from Spain to become the new ruler of the California territory.

1846 ► U.S. declares war against Mexico.

In Sonoma, American settlers successfully attack Mexican authorities during the Bear Flag Revolt. Their newly formed Republic of California lasts less than a month. The Bear Flaggers later join the U.S. in its efforts to make California a state.

1848 ► The Gold Rush begins when James Marshall discovers gold in Coloma.

California becomes a U.S. Territory with the Treaty of Guadalupe, and the end of the Mexican-American War.

1850 ► **September 9,** California is admitted into the Union as the 31st state.

The 'whip', **Charlie Parkhurst** drives her coach over every road near the Mother Lode.

Chinese immigrants migrate to California in large numbers to labor in gold mining camps.

1851 ► **Dame Shirley** chronicles life in two gold mining camps.

1856 ► **Biddy Mason** sues for and wins freedom from slavery.

1864 ► **Juana Briones** wins a court case giving her sole title to her property holdings.

1870 ► The Economy slows. Chinese are seen as a threat to American jobs.

1882 ► The U.S. passes the Chinese Exclusion Act, which bars all Chinese immigration to the U.S. The law will not be repealed for another sixty years.

1910 ► Angel Island opens. For the next thirty years, it serves as point of entry to the United States for Asian immigrants. Some Asians will wait on the island for up to two years before being 'processed' for entry to the U.S.

1911 ► The Millionaire Waitress, **Maud Younger,** sees the payoff for her efforts to enact women's suffrage and fair labor laws. California grants voting rights to its women.

1916 ► **Ruth Law** breaks three distance flying records.

1929 ► The Wall Street Crash of 1929 marks the beginning of The Great Depression. **Dorothea Lange** begins photographing the unemployed and homeless that result from this economic downturn.

1941 ► December 7, Japan bombs Pearl Harbor. The next day, the U.S. enters World War II.

1942 ► President Franklin Roosevelt signs Executive Order 9066. Thousands of Japanese Americans, including **Sox Kitashima**, are sent to internment camps for the rest of the war.

1940s ► Laying the groundwork for future civil rights movements, **Charlotta Bass** campaigns for equal property ownership rights.

1948 ► President Harry Truman signs into law the Japanese-American Claims Act. Total damages reach $131 million for which only $38 million will be paid to survivors of internment camps -- and to their heirs.

1965 ► **Dolores Huerta** helps direct the United Farm Workers' grape boycott.

1973 ► **Billy Jean King** defeats Bobby Riggs in a tennis match dubbed the Battle of the Sexes.

1974 ► Nixon resigns in disgrace. Gerald Ford becomes President of the U.S. **Betty Ford** becomes First Lady.

1983 ► **Sally Ride** becomes the first American woman in space on the Space Shuttle *Challenger*.

1986 ► Olympic bronze medalist, **Anita DeFrantz** becomes the first woman and first African American to represent the U.S. on the International Olympic Committee.

2003 ► Arnold Schwarzenegger is elected to replace Governor Gray Davis. **Maria Shriver** becomes First Lady of California.

2006 ► **Nancy Pelosi** becomes the first woman, first Californian, and first Italian-American to be elected Speaker of the House.

Author/Writer Credits

"Maud Younger: Millionaire Waitress," "Dorothea Lange: Changing the World Through Photography," and "Dian Fossey: Protector of the Mountain Gorilla" © 2009 by Linda Crotta Brennan.

"Louisa A.K.S. Clappe: 'Dame Shirley' of the Gold Rush," "Mabel Fairbanks: Skater Breaks the Ice Barrier," Tsuyako 'Sox' Kitashima: Righting the Wrongs for Japanese Americans," and "Anita L. DeFrantz: Olympian" © 2009 by Deborah Bruss

"Ruth Law: Daring Aviator" © 2009 by Janet Buell

"Jessie Anne Frémont: Explorer's Wife and Writer," "Charlotta S. Bass: Journalist and Activist," "Betty Ford: First Lady of the United States," "Dolores Huerta: Activist for Migrant Workers" and "Billie Jean King: Tennis Ace and Activist" © 2009 by Marty Darragh

"Juana Briones: One of San Francisco's First Residents," "Charlotte 'Charlie' Parkhurst: Legendary Stagecoach Driver," "Bridget 'Biddy' Mason: Freed Slave, Wealthy Landowner, Philanthropist," and "Sally Ride: First Woman Astronaut" © 2009 by Kathleen W. Deady

"Nancy Pelosi: First Woman Speaker of the House" © 2009 by M. Lu Major

"Maxine Hong Kingston: Writer of the Chinese American Experience" © 2009 by Diane Mayr

"Maria Shriver: Journalist and First Lady of California" © 2009 by Andrea Murphy

"Alice Eastwood: Plant Pioneer," "Janice Mirikitani: Word Warrior," and "Judith Baca: Healing with Art:" © 2009 Joyce Ray

"Ethel Percy Andrus: A Life of Service to Others" © 2009 Patty Lyman Schremmer

"Marcy Carsey: TV Producer" © 2009 Sally Wilkins

Photo and Illustration Credits

pages 7, 12, & 22 Illustrations by Lisa Greenleaf

page 9, Courtesy of Juana Briones Foundation

page 14, Courtesy of Legends of America

page 17, Granger Collection/New York

page 24, Courtesy of California State Library

page 29, Courtesy of Benecke Library/Yale

pages 32 & 34, Courtesy of California Academy of Science

pages cover/37, 39, 52, 57, 59 & 67 Library of Congress

pages 42 & 44, Photograph courtesy of the Southern California Library for Social Studies and Research

pages 47 & 49, Courtesy of AARP

page 54, Courtesy of Missouri State Archives

page 64, Courtesy of vieilles_annonces/Flickr.com

page 69, Courtesy of Gerald R. Ford Library

page 72, Courtesy of Ted Kurihara

page 74, Courtesy of Isao Tanaka

pages 77/cover, Courtesy of Angela Torres/Dolores Huerta Foundation

page 79, Estuary Print

pages 82 & 84, Courtesy of Gorilla Fund

page 87/cover, Courtesy of Gail Evenari

page 89, Random House

pages 92 &94, Courtesy of House of Representatives

pages 97 & 99, Courtesy of Janice Mirikitani

page 102, Wikipedia.com

page 104, Getty Images Sport

page 107, Mark Mainz /Getty Images

pages 112 & 114, Courtesy of SPARCA

pages 117 &119, Courtesy of NASA

page 122, Kirby Lee/Getty Images

page 124, Courtesy of International Olympic Committee

page 127, Getty Images Entertainment, Maria Shriver

page 129, Courtesy of the Office of the Governor (California)

Table of Contents

— 1 —
Juana Briones:
One of San Francisco's First Residents

by Kathleen W. Deady

*J*uana had tolerated her husband's drinking. She had supported their family when he had not. But she would not take his beatings any longer. The authorities had not helped her. In 1836, women had few rights or protections.

So Juana packed their belongings and left. Juana was strong. She would manage. She had to. She had seven children depending on her.

· · · · ৩৩ · · · ·

Juana was born around 1802 in Villa Branciforte, now Santa Cruz. She was in the first generation of her family to be born in California. Her grandparents had lived in New Spain, now Mexico. They wanted a better life. In 1776, when Juana's mother was just four, they traveled 1600 miles to settle in California.

Juana's mother later married a soldier from the **Mission** Santa Cruz. In 1797, they helped found Branciforte. It was here that Juana was born.

Juana was of mixed European, African, and Native American descent.

•◆•

Juana and Apolinario eventually had eleven children. Seven survived. Juana also raised an orphaned Indian girl.

•◆•

Juana was one of the first residents in Yerba Buena. This new **pueblo** was named for the wild mint that covered the area. It would later be renamed San Francisco.

Growing up was not easy for Juana. The **padres** at the mission were very strict. Juana also had no school to attend. However, her mother and the natives taught her many things. She learned especially about healing and **herbal** medicines.

Around 1812, Juana's mother died. The family moved to the Presidio. This military village was used for farming and grazing livestock. Many of the soldiers drank and bullied others. At about 18, Juana married a soldier named Apolinario Miranda.

Juana ran their household and raised their children. However, her marriage was unhappy. Her husband drank a lot. He did little farming or ranching.

Juana struggled to support the family. She sold food to sailors docked nearby. She treated sailors for **scurvy.** She hid those who left their ships to escape horrible conditions.

In 1833, Juana and her husband got another plot of land nearby. Juana raised cattle and developed fruit tree orchards. But her husband was becoming abusive. In those days, a divorce was difficult to get and illegal in the Catholic Church.

Finally, around 1836, Juana left her husband. She settled on a plot of land at Yerba Buena, now North Beach in San Francisco. Her husband tried to force her to come back. Juana got the justice of the peace to order him to stay away.

Juana built a prosperous business. She sold fresh meat and farmed vegetables to support her family. She used her knowledge of healing and medicines to help people. She fixed broken bones and delivered babies. Juana became well known in the area as a healer and **midwife**.

In 1844, Juana paid $300 for a 4400-acre ranch for her growing business. However, she was still married. By law, her husband could sell what she owned. Juana told her church that she alone had earned everything she had. She got a legal separation to protect her land and money.

Around 1847, Juana's husband died. In 1852, she learned that the government was planning to take her lands. It did not think her separation was legal.

Many women in her position could have lost everything. But Juana fought back in court. She had many legal documents, contracts, and maps about her business dealings. Her case went to the Supreme Court. After 12 years, Juana finally won. She kept her land and independence until her death in 1889.

Juana was raised in a culture where women had few rights. But her strength and success made her a role model for women then and now.

TIDBITS

Juana often refused to take payment from people who were sick. "If they get well, I am satisfied," she said.

• ◆ •

Juana could not read or write. Trusted friends read legal documents for her. She signed her name with an X.

• ◆ •

Juana owned five properties in her life.

• ◆ •

A park and a school in Palo Alto are named after Juana.

The remains of the Juana Briones House.

Timeline: Juana Briones

1802 ► Juana Briones born in Villa Branciforte, now Santa Cruz to Maria Ysiadora Tapia, and Marcos Briones.

1812 ► Juana's mother dies, the family moves to Mission Dolores, on the grounds of El Presidio de San Francisco.

1820 ► May, she marries Apolinario Miranda, a 27 year old cavalryman stationed at the Presidio. They soon join her sister Guadalupe's family in El Polin Springs. Juana and Apolinario eventually have 11 children. Four do not survive infancy.

1833 ► Juana and her husband obtain a land grant for a site they call El Ojo de Agua do Figueroa.

1834 ► Juana travels to Marin Country to help with an outbreak of smallpox.

c1836 ► She leaves her husband and settles a plot of land in a new pueblo called Yerba Buena, now North Beach in San Francisco.

For the next five years, Juana lives alternately between El Polin Springs, El Ojo de Agua de Figueroa, and Yerba Buena.

1844 ► Juana buys a 4400-acre tract called Rancho La Purisima Concepcion in present day Palo Alto and Los Altos Hills. She continues to develop a growing cattle business. She obtains a legal separation from her husband to protect her rights and investments.

c1847 ► Her husband Apolinario dies.

1852 ► Juana buys land in Santa Clara.

She learns the government does not consider her separation legal and plans to take her land.

c1864 ► Juana wins her court case and secures legal rights to her land for the rest of her life.

1884 ► She buys a house in Mayfield, now part of Palo Alto, to be close to her daughter. By now Juana is suffering from arthritis.

1889 ► December 3, Juana dies. She is buried in Holy Cross Cemetery in Menlo Park.

1997 ► October 5, the State Department honors her with a plaque in Washington Square in San Francisco, near where her Yerba Buena home was 150 years before.

NOTE: c1836 means about or around 1836

Learn More about Juana Briones and Early California History

- Furbee, Mary Rodd. *Outrageous Women of the American Frontier.* John Wiley & Sons, Inc. 2002.

- Pelz, Ruth. *Women of the Wild West: Biographies from Many Cultures.* Open Hand Publishing, Inc. 1995.

- Richter, Glenda. *The Story of Juana Briones: Alta California Pioneer.* Bookhandler Press, 2002.

Web sites:

- Juana Briones' life:
  www.brioneshouse.org/juanas_life.htm

- Presidio of San Francisco: Juana Briones:
  http://www.nps.gov/prsf/historyculture/juana-briones.htm

Glossary

herbal (UR buhl) Made with herbs, plants used for cooking or medicine.

midwife (MID wife) A person who assists women in childbirth.

mission (MISH uhn) A group of buildings, usually including a church, where religious teachers work and live.

padres (PAH drayz) A Spanish word meaning "fathers." The name given to Catholic priests.

pueblo (PWEB loh) Buildings made of adobe or stone built next to and on top of each other to create a village.

scurvy (SKUR vee) A disease that causes weakness and bleeding gums. It occurs when a person does not get enough Vitamin C. Sailors on long sea voyages often got scurvy because they did not get fresh fruits and vegetables to eat.

— 2 —
Charlotte "Charlie" Parkhurst:
Legendary Stagecoach Driver

by Kathleen W. Deady

Old Charlie Parkhurst, one of the best stagecoach drivers ever, was dead. He had told his friends he wanted to be buried as he had lived, in his dirty old clothes. But the townspeople insisted on cleaning him up for burial. When they undressed him, they got the shock of their lives.

Charlie was a woman! How had she hidden her **identity** her whole life? And why?

· · · · ⟲ · · · ·

Charlie was born Charlotte Darkey Parkhurst in 1812 in Lebanon, New Hampshire. Much about Charlie's life is not known for sure. Over the years, people have guessed at many details.

Charlie grew up mostly in an **orphanage**. Her parents had either died or abandoned her when she was very young. In her early teens, Charlie ran away from the orphanage dressed as a boy. A girl could not have gotten work in those days. However, a boy might become an **apprentice** and learn a business.

Charlie found work at a **livery** stable in Worcester, Massachusetts. The owner, Ebenezer Balch, gave Charlie room, board, and a job as a stable boy. Balch saw Charlie's natural ability with horses. Over time, he trained Charlie to drive coaches and carriages. Charlie became a very skilled and safe driver.

In the early 1840s, Charlie moved with Balch to Providence, Rhode Island. She soon became a popular driver around the area. People often insisted on having only Charlie as their driver.

Before long, Charlie moved to Georgia. She worked for Jim Birch and Frank Stevens. By 1849, the Gold Rush had begun in California. Birch and Stevens headed west to operate the California Stage Company. Charlie soon followed.

Through the 1850s and 1860s, Charlie drove nearly every route in California. Driving stage in the Wild West was very dangerous. Mountain roads were often winding and steep. Narrow turns with 1000-foot drop-offs were common. Coaches could crash head-on at curves or tumble over the edge. Indians and outlaws were also a constant danger. Yet Charlie was known as the fastest and safest driver in California.

How did Charlie fit in as a man? She was around 5'7" with a slight build. Unlike the men, she had no beard. However, she drank, chewed tobacco, smoked cigars, and swore like men. She wore blue jeans and a loose pleated shirt to cover her female figure. She also wore a wide brimmed hat, and sometimes a buffalo hide coat. And year round, she wore buckskin gloves, probably to cover her small hands. With this disguise, no one suspected she was not a man.

TIDBITS

Charlie did many good deeds, including donating money to needy causes.

◆

An outlaw named Sugarfoot once robbed Charlie. Charlie vowed it would never happen again. She learned to shoot a 44 pistol. The next time Sugarfoot tried, Charlie shot him dead.

◆

Charlie had several nicknames, including One-Eyed Charlie, Mountain Charlie, and Six-Horse Charlie.

By the late 1860s, Charlie was suffering from **rheumatism**, a common problem for drivers. Trains were also expanding. Charlie quit driving and opened a stage station and saloon between Santa Cruz and Watsonville. Later she worked in lumbering, cattle ranching, and chicken farming.

For a few years, Charlie lived alone near Watsonville. She was in poor health, but refused medical treatment. In 1879, Charlie died of cancer of the tongue. It was then her secret was revealed and she became famous. People started telling stories about her life. Some were true. Many were exaggerated. But the stories made Charlie a **legend**.

Why had Charlie lived her life as a man? No one really knows. Probably, the **disguise** gave her the freedom to do the driving she loved. One thing is certain. Charlie had strength, courage, and an independent spirit. She had just what was needed in the American West.

Stages coaches like this one were the main transportation in the early west.

Timeline: Charlotte "Charlie" Parkhurst

1812 ➤ Born Charlotte Darkey Parkhurst in Lebanon, New Hampshire. She grows up mainly in an orphanage in New Hampshire or Massachusetts.

Mid 1820s ➤ She dresses as a boy and runs away from the orphanage. Finds job as stable boy for Ebenezer Balch, keeper of an inn and livery stable in Worcester, Massachusetts.

Early 1840s ➤ Charlie moves to Providence, Rhode Island with Balch and works for him in What Cheer Stables for a year or two. In high demand as a driver.

Mid 1840s ➤ Charlie moves to Georgia, works for Jim Birch and Frank Stephens.

1849 ➤ She returns briefly to Rhode Island when Birch and Stephens leave for California at the start of Gold Rush.

1851 ➤ Charlie arrives in California.

Early 1850s ➤ Charlie is kicked by the horse she is shoeing, loses the sight in her left eye and starts wearing a patch, gets the nickname One-Eyed Charlie.

Drives coaches through some of the wildest **boom towns**, including Rough and Ready, Grass Valley, and Placerville.

Mid 1850s ➤ Charlie drives new routes from Oakland to San Juan Boulista.

1856 ➤ Lives at Searsville in San Mateo City.

1860s ➤ Highly respected driver in the state. Often trusted to drive special missions for Wells Fargo.

Late 1860s ➤ Retires from driving, opens a stage station and saloon. Later works in cattle ranching and lumbering.

1868 ➤ Registers and probably votes in presidential election between Horatio Seymour and Ulysses S. Grant, one year before any territory or state allowed women to vote, and five decades before women could vote nationwide.

1879 ➤ Around December 29, Charlie dies in her cabin near Watsonville, California of cancer of the tongue. Is buried in Pioneer Odd Fellows Cemetery in Watsonville.

Later, town of Soquel honors Charlie with bronze plaque as " . . . the first woman in the world to vote in a presidential election (November 4, 1868)."

Learn More about Charlie Parkhurst, Stagecoaches, and the Wild West

- Furbee, Mary Rodd. *Outrageous Women of the American Frontier.* John Wiley and Sons, Inc., 2002.

- Kay, Verla. *Rough Tough Charlie.* Tricycle Press, 2007.

- Ryan, Pam Munoz. *Riding Freedom.* Scholastic Press, 1998.

Web sites:

- Stagecoach Days 2008: Get On Board:
  http://www.parks.ca.gov/?page_id = 25066

- Famous Women of the Wild West, and other good information:
  http://www.outlawwomen.com/famous_women_of_the_wild_west.htm

Glossary

apprentice (uh PREN tiss) Someone who learns a trade or craft by working with a skilled person.

boom town (BOOM toun) A town that grows quickly because of the nearby discovery of a resource such as oil or gold.

disguise (diss GIZE) A type of dress that hides a person's identity.

identity (eye DEN ti tee) Who a person really is.

legend (LEJ uhnd) A story handed down from earlier times, often based on fact.

livery (LIV ur ee) A stable where horses are taken care of for a fee.

orphanage (OR fuh nij) A place where orphans live and are looked after

rheumatism (ROO muh TIZ uhm) A disease that causes the joints and muscles to become swollen, stiff, and painful.

— 3 —
Bridget "Biddy" Mason:
Freed Slave, Wealthy Landowner, Philanthropist

by Kathleen W. Deady

*B*iddy stood in the Los Angeles courtroom. She listened to the decision of Judge Benjamin Hayes.

"In the matter of Biddy . . . on this nineteenth day of January [1856] . . . all persons of color cannot be held in slavery . . . and are forever free."

Biddy rejoiced. Those words meant a new life. She had no home or job. But she had skills and friends. Most important, she had strength, determination, and dreams.

· · · · ◠◡ · · · ·

Biddy was born into slavery on August 15, 1818, probably in Georgia. She was given the name Bridget but had no last name. Biddy was separated from her parents as a young child.

In 1836, Biddy was either sold or given as a wedding gift to Robert and Rebecca Smith. Like most slaves, Biddy had not been allowed to learn to read or write. However, she had learned many good skills from the other

The trip to Utah took seven months. Biddy herded the cattle, prepared meals, and cared for her children. She also delivered several babies along the way.

• ◆ •

Biddy and Smith's other slaves were jailed during the court case. This action kept them safe so Smith could not take them from the state.

• ◆ •

Biddy's court case happened nine years before the Thirteenth Amendment abolished slavery in America.

slaves, especially as a nurse and **midwife**. During the next 12 years, Biddy had three daughters. Robert Smith was believed to be their father.

In 1848, Biddy and her children moved with Smith to the Utah Territory. Smith had **converted** to the **Mormon** religion. He wanted to join a new center in Salt Lake City. The trip was over 2000 miles. Biddy and the other slaves walked the whole way behind the wagons and livestock.

In 1851, Biddy moved again with Smith to California. Smith probably did not know that California had become a free state in 1850. Slavery was no longer legal. And Biddy could not know the trip would bring her closer to freedom.

At first, no one questioned slave owners. But by 1855, the new laws were being more strictly enforced. Smith decided to move to Texas where slavery was still legal. Biddy had friends who were freed slaves. They helped her **petition** the court for her freedom. On January 19, 1856, the court granted Biddy's request.

At 37, Biddy was free for the first time in her life. She took the last name Mason and moved to Los Angeles. Biddy got a job as a nurse and midwife. She earned $2.50 a day.

Biddy soon became well known for her kindness. She delivered babies for many families. She made **herbal remedies**. In the 1860s, **smallpox** hit Los Angeles. Biddy risked her own life to help many sick people. She never cared what color someone was. She simply helped anyone in need.

By 1866, she had saved $250. Biddy bought two lots of land

on the edge of town. She built small homes on her land and rented them for extra income. As her income grew, Biddy sold some land for profit and bought more.

Biddy understood that land could increase in value. She planned well and made good investments. Los Angeles developed quickly. By the late 1800s, the area was the center of the **financial district**. Her land was worth a lot of money.

Biddy lived simply and used her growing wealth to help others. She gave shelter in her home to anyone who needed it. She donated money to schools, churches, and day care centers. She visited prisons and hospitals to offer gifts and comfort.

Biddy became very wealthy. However, she was most famous for her generosity. She once said, "If you hold your hands closed . . . nothing good can come in. The open hand is blessed, for it gives in abundance, even as it receives."

Biddy died January 15, 1891 at 72 years old. She was buried as she had lived, simply, in an unmarked grave. Nearly 100 years later, the city of Los Angeles honored Biddy. The mayor placed a tombstone at her grave site.

TIDBITS

Biddy was one of the first African American women to own property in California. She called her first piece of land her **homestead.**

◆

People of all races came to Biddy's home for help. Many called her "Grandma Mason."

◆

During severe flooding in the 1880s, many people lost their homes. Biddy opened accounts at grocery stores and paid for anything they needed.

Timeline: Bridget "Biddy" Mason

1818 ➤ August 15, born into slavery, probably in Hancock County, Georgia, of mixed African American and Native American descent. Never knew her parents or their names.

1836 ➤ Sold or given to Robert and Rebecca Smith of Mississippi as a wedding present.

1838 ➤ October 15, gives birth to first child, a daughter Ellen. Later has two more daughters, Anne (1844) and Harriet (1848).

1848 ➤ March 10, Biddy and her daughters leave Mississippi for Salt Lake City, Utah with Robert Smith, and group of 56 whites and 34 slaves.

1850 ➤ September, California joins the Union as a free state.

1851 ➤ Travels with Smith from Utah Territory to Bernadino, California.

Early 1850's ➤ Learns of possibility of freedom from friends, including Robert Owens and his son Charles. Daughter Ellen later marries Charles.

1855 ➤ Smith plans to move. Owens convinces sheriff to stop Smith from taking slaves to Texas, which still allows slavery.

1856 ➤ January 19, Judge Benjamin Hayes frees Biddy and the rest of Smith's slaves. Biddy takes the last name Mason. Moves with daughters to Los Angeles.

1860s ➤ Biddy risks her life caring for people during small pox epidemic.

1866 ➤ November 28, buys first two lots of land on edge of town with money she has saved.

1880s ➤ Buys food and supplies for flood victims.

1884 ➤ Sells part of land for $1500. Builds **commercial** building with rental spaces on rest of land. Moves into second floor with her family.

Late 1800s ➤ Becomes wealthiest woman in Los Angeles, worth almost $300,000.

1891 ➤ January 15, dies, is buried in unmarked grave in Evergreen Cemetery in Los Angeles.

1988 ➤ March 27, Los Angeles mayor Tom Bradley, lays tombstone at her grave site.

1989 ➤ November 16 is declared Biddy Mason Day in Los Angeles.

Learn More about Bridget "Biddy" Mason and Slavery

- Furbee, Mary Rodd. *Outrageous Women of the American Frontier.* John Wiley & Sons, Inc., 2002.

- Kamma, Anne and Pamela Johnson. *If You Lived When There Was Slavery in America.* Scholastic, 2004.

- Williams, Jean Kinney. *Bridget "Biddy" Mason: From Slave To Businesswoman.* Compass Point Books, 2005.

Web sites:

- Mason, Bridget "Biddy" (1818-1891):
  http://www.blackpast.org/?q = aaw/mason-bridget-biddy-1818-1891

- Women in History: Biddy Mason:
  http://www.lkwdpl.org/wihohio/maso-bid.htm

Glossary

commercial (kuh MUR shuhl) Something that will make money.

converted (kuhn VURT id) Changed or made into something else.

financial district (fye NAN shuhl DISS trict) The part of a town where most of the banks are located.

herbal remedies (URB uhl REM uh deez) Medicines made from herbs and other natural products.

homestead (HOME stead) A farmhouse and all its other buildings and land.

midwife (MID wife) A person who helps women in childbirth.

Mormon (MOR muhn) One who belongs to the Church of Jesus Christ of Latter-day Saints.

petition (puh TISH uhn) To asked people in power to change a rule or action.

smallpox (SMAWL poks) A serious and contagious disease that causes fever and pimples that can leave permanent scars on a person's body.

— 4 —
Louise A.K.S. Clappe:
"Dame Shirley" of the Gold Rush

by Deborah Bruss

September 20, 1851

Louise Clapp hiked up her long skirt and **petticoats** to keep them from dragging in the mud. She walked past crude cabins and tents in the mining camp. One miner's shelter consisted of pine **boughs** covered with old **calico** shirts.

Louise was going to see her husband, Dr. Clapp. He'd boasted about his new office.

Later that day, Louise wrote a long letter to her sister about her visit. "When I entered this imposing place the shock… was so great that I sank helplessly upon one of the benches, which ran… the whole length (ten feet!) of the building, and laughed till I cried. There was, of course, no floor…. The shelves… looked like sticks snatched hastily from the wood-pile…."

· · · · ⌒⊙ · · · ·

Very few women lived in the gold mining camps of California. Louise was one of them. She wrote 23 letters to her sister, Molly, who lived in Massachusetts. They gave many details - serious and humorous - about life during the California Gold Rush. She signed her letters, "Dame Shirley."

Louise Smith was born in New Jersey in 1819. Her father died when she was 13, and her mother died five years later. Louise and her sister, Molly, went to live with their **guardian** in Amherst, Massachusetts. Louise attended college, studied French, German and Italian, and traveled a lot.

Louise married a medical student, Fayette Clapp. They wanted to join the gold rush excitement in California. In 1849, they sailed around the tip of South America to San Francisco.

Louise loved the hilly city. It was alive with **adventurous** people. But the foggy weather was bad for Dr. Clapp's health. In 1851 they moved to the mountains.

The journey was dangerous. They got lost. They heard the snuffling of grizzly bears while sleeping under the stars. Louise wrote, "Fancy yourself riding…along the edge of a frightful **precipice**… should your mule make a misstep, you would be dashed hundreds of feet into the awful ravine below."

At the mining camp, Rich Bar, Louise wrote about the women who lived there. One was called Indiana Girl. "This gentle creature wears the thickest pair of miner's boots…. Last spring she… packed fifty pounds of flour on her back down that awful hill – the snow being five feet deep at the time."

The following spring, the Clapps moved upriver to Indian

TIDBITS

Louise washed a pan of dirt and found $3.25 worth of gold dust and mailed it to her sister with a letter that said, "…I wet my feet, tore my dress, spoilt a pair of new gloves, nearly froze my fingers, got an awful headache… in this labor of love. I can assure you that it is the last golden handiwork you will ever receive from Dame Shirley."

TIDBITS

Going to see the elephant was a saying used during that time. It meant, to travel west and try one's luck at finding gold.

•◆•

No one knows why Louise chose the pen name, *Dame Shirley*.

•◆•

After her divorce from Fayette, she added an "e" to the end of her last name and became Louise Clappe.

Bar. Louise wrote about **gruesome** mining accidents, murders, thefts and a hanging. She told about the death of a woman and her "sickly babe ten months old, which was moaning **piteously** for its mother." She described "Mrs. R," who earned $100 per week by washing miners' clothes with her "tiny hands."

The Clapps dreaded spending another winter on the Feather River. Yet, when it was time to leave, Louise wrote, "My heart is heavy at the thought of departing forever from this place. I like this wild and **barbarous** life…."

They returned to San Francisco, but Fayette didn't stay long. Later they divorced. Louise remained there and became one of the city's first teachers. A few years later, a magazine published all of Louise's letters. She retired in 1878 and moved to New York. She died in 1906.

In 1922, the letters were published in a book, *The Shirley Letters: From the California Mines, 1851-1852*.

These letters tell us a lot about life in the gold mining camps and towns – especially the life of one very brave woman.

There were few women living in the early California mining towns.

Timeline: Louise A. K. S. Clappe

1819 ▶ July 28, Louise Amelia Knapp Smith is born in Elizabethtown, NJ to Moses Smith and Lois Lee. She is the oldest of seven children.

1832 ▶ Louise's father dies.

1837 ▶ Her mother dies. She and her sister, Molly, move to Amherst, MA. They live with their guardian and friend of the family, Osmyn Baker.

1837–1848 ▶ Louise goes to college in Massachusetts and travels to many places on the east coast.

1848 ▶ Louise marries Fayette Clapp, a 24-year-old medical student.
Gold is discovered on the American River in California.

1849 ▶ The California Gold Rush begins. In August, Louise and her husband board a boat bound for California, where he plans to be a doctor.

1850 ▶ Louise and her husband arrive in San Francisco after more than five months at sea.
Two men find a chunk of gold on the Feather River. In two weeks they take out $6000 worth of gold. Soon 500 men arrive and settle in a camp called Rich Bar.

1851 ▶ Louise and Fayette move to Rich Bar, about 120 miles northeast of Sacramento in the Sierra Nevada. A few months later they move upriver to Indian Bar.

1852 ▶ Louise and Fayette return to San Francisco after spending one and a half years in the mining camps.

1855–56 ▶ Louise's letters are published in *The Pioneer*, California's first magazine, under the pen name, "Dame Shirley."

1857 ▶ Fayette returns to Massachusetts. Louise becomes one of San Francisco's first teachers.

1878 ▶ She retires from teaching and moves to New York City, where she writes and gives lectures.

1906 ▶ Louise dies at age 87 in NJ.

1922 ▶ *The Shirley Letters From California Mines in 1851-52* are published as a book.

Learn More About Louise Clappe and the Women in the California Gold Rush

- Rawls, James J. *Dame Shirley and the Gold Rush (Stories of America).* Steck-Vaughn, 1992.
- Cushman, Karen. *The Ballad of Lucy Whipple.* HarperTrophy, 1999.
- Gregory, Kristiana K. *Seeds of Hope: The Gold Rush Diary of Susanna Fairchild, California Territory 1849 (Dear America Series).* Scholastic, 2003.
- Krohn, Katherine E. *Women of the Wild West.* Lerner Publishing Group, 2000.

Web sites:

- Gold Rush web site:
  http://www.calgoldrush.com/
- A Lady's Life in the Gold Rush:
  http://www.historynet.com/a-ladys-life-in-the-gold-rush.htm
- "Dame Shirley" Describes Life at a California Gold Mining Camp:
  http://historymatters.gmu.edu/d/6516/
- Oakland Museum of California Interactive Web site about the Gold Rush:
  http://www.museumca.org/goldrush/
- The Virtual Museum of the City of San Francisco, links to the Gold Rush:
  http://www.sfmuseum.org/hist1/index0.1.html#gold

Glossary

adventurous (ad VEN chur uhss) Looking for exciting or dangerous experiences.

barbarous (BAR bur uhss) Untamed and rough.

bough (BOU) A thick branch of a tree.

calico (KAL I KOH) Cotton cloth printed with colorful patterns.

gruesome (GROO suhm) Disgusting and horrible.

guardian (GAR dee uhn) Someone, other than a parent, who has the legal responsibility to look after a child.

petticoats (PET ee KOHTSS) Thin garments worn under a skirt or dress; a slip.

piteously (PIT ee uhss lee) In a sad, pitiful way.

precipice (PRESS uh piss) A steep cliff.

Jessie Anne Frémont:
Explorer's Wife & Writer

by Marty Darragh

*J*essie hated Miss English's Female **Seminary**. The principal wrote to her father, "Miss Jessie although extremely intelligent, lacks the **docility** of a model student. Moreover, she has the objectionable manner of seeming to take our orders and assignments under consideration, to be accepted or disregarded by some standard of her own."

The rest of her life was marked by standards of her own.

· · · · ☾☽ · · · ·

Jessie Anne Benton was born May 31, 1824. Jessie's father was the powerful Missouri Senator, Thomas Hart Benton. Her mother, Elizabeth McDowell, was a strong-willed Southern belle. Jessie was the second of seven children. She was named for her father's parents, Jesse and Anne Benton.

Even though sons came later, Jessie's father treated her as if she were a boy. She accompanied him when he went to the White House and to his

Jessie could read by age 4. In her teens she spoke 5 languages and could read Latin and Greek.

•—•—•

Jessie's mother, Elizabeth, inherited forty slaves. Elizabeth freed them all in the 1830s. This action laid the foundation of Jessie's anti-slavery beliefs.

•—•—•

To get to California, Jessie traveled by steamship to a port on the Caribbean Sea in Panama. Then she used a boat, canoe, and mule to cross the **isthmus** to get to Panama City.

office at the Capitol. At a desk in the corner of his library, she listened to political discussions between her father and visitors.

Her life changed at 14. She and her sister, Eliza, were sent to a boarding school in Georgetown. When Jessie was 15, the handsome and adventurous John C. Frémont entered her life. He was an Army lieutenant with the **Topographical** Engineers. Senator Benton befriended the explorer.

One night, John escorted Jessie's younger sister to a concert at Miss English's school. There he met Jessie. It has been said that it was love at first sight. Her father was alarmed at the obvious romance. He arranged for John to go on an exploration. The separation didn't work. John and Jessie secretly married when she turned 17.

Jessie was John's strongest supporter. She helped write his popular reports after expeditions. She added descriptive words and varied the language. Jessie answered John's correspondence. She even signed his name. When he got in trouble for refusing to obey orders, she rushed to help. She went to see Presidents on his behalf.

In 1849, John and Jessie moved to California. Jessie went by way of Panama to meet John. Gold was discovered on their ranch. They became millionaires.

Jessie wrote her first book some years later, during the Civil War. She gave all the profits to charity.

John was never a good businessman. He did not pay attention to his mining interests in California. He lost everything. By

1873, the Frémonts had no money. Jessie took up writing again and supported the family.

When John became sick, his doctor ordered him to go to Los Angeles. Jessie continued to support the family with her writing. After recovering, John went to Washington. He rejoined the Army and received a **pension** of $6,000 per year.

John died before he could return to California. Jessie sent a telegram to their son, Charley. She asked him to put the miniature portrait of her in John's hands before he was buried.

John had many debts. The country found out about Jessie's financial problems. Congress voted her a small pension. Jessie was a friend of many leaders of the California **Federation** of Women's Clubs but had never been a member. When they learned Jessie was in need, club members raised money to buy land and build her a house.

The well-traveled and adventurous woman died peacefully in her sleep on December 27, 1902.

TIDBITS

John and Jessie Frémont had 5 children. Two died in infancy.

•◆•

John ran for president in 1856 and Jessie actively campaigned for him. She was the first candidate's wife to do so.

•◆•

In 1873, Jessie was paid $100 for each article she wrote for the *New York Ledger*.

When the Frémonts lost all of their money, Jessie supported the family with her writing.

Timeline: Jessie Anne Frémont

1824 ➤ May 31, Jessie Anne is born at Cherry Grove, her grandparents' estate in Virginia. Her parents are Elizabeth Preston McDowell and Thomas Hart Benton.

1841 ➤ October 19, she **elopes** with John C. Frémont.

1842 ➤ May 2, John leaves to lead his first expedition.

November 15, daughter Elizabeth (Lily) is born.

1843 ➤ John leaves from St. Louis for his second expedition.

1845–1847 ➤ John leads his third expedition to California. He fights in the Mexican War. He faces a court martial for refusing to obey an order.

1848 ➤ July 24, son Benton is born. Dies 10 weeks later.

1849 ➤ March 15, Jessie and Lily start for California.

Gold is discovered on the Frémont ranch.

1850 ➤ John is elected one of the first two senators from the new state of California. His term is for only one year. The Frémonts return to Washington, D.C.

1851 ➤ April 19, son John Charles (Charley) is born.

1852 ➤ The Frémonts travel to England and France.

1853 ➤ February 1, daughter Anne Beverly is born in Paris. She dies 5 months later.

1855 ➤ May 17, Jessie's last child, Francis Preston Blair (Frank) is born.

1856 ➤ John runs for President as the first Republican candidate. The party has an anti-slavery **platform**. John loses to James Buchanan.

1861 ➤ President Lincoln names John head of the Western Department stationed in St. Louis. At Jessie's urging he frees the slaves in Missouri, upsetting Lincoln and his Civil War **strategies.**

1873 ➤ Poor business skills and lack of attention cost the Frémonts everything. Jessie takes over supporting the family with her writing.

1877 ➤ John is appointed governor of Arizona Territory.

1888 ➤ The Frémonts settle in Los Angeles.

1890 ➤ John dies in New York.

1902 ➤ Jessie dies in Los Angeles.

Learn More about Jessie Frémont and Western Exploration

- Anderson, Dale. *Westward Expansion.* Raintree Steck-Vaughn, 2001.
- Morrison, Dorothy Nafus. *Under a Strong Wind: The Adventures of Jessie Benton Frémont.* Atheneum, 1983.
- Randall, Ruth Painter. *I Jessie: A Biography of the Girl Who Married John Charles Frémont Famous Explorer of the West.* Little, Brown & Company, 1963.
- Souza, D. M. *John C. Frémont.* Franklin Watts, 2004.

Web sites:

- An Overview of Mariposa County History:
  http://www.visitmariposa.net/history.htm
- Jessie Benton Frémont plans Christmas in California:
  http://www.explorehistoricalif.com/jessie_xmas_fairyland.html

Glossary

docility (daw SIL i tee) Calmness, easily led.

elope (i LOPE) To run away to get married.

federation (FED uh RAY shuhn) A group joined together by an agreement or common cause.

isthmus (ISS muhss) A narrow strip of land that lies between two bodies of water and connects two larger land masses. The country of Panama is an isthmus that connects North and South America.

pension (PEN shuhn) An amount of money paid regularly to someone.

platform (PLAT form) The statement of beliefs of a political party.

seminary (SEM uh NER ee) In the 1800s, a girls' high school or boarding school.

strategies (STRAT uh geez) Plans for winning a battle or achieving a goal.

topographical (tawp uh GRAF uh kuhl) Having to do with the exact description of an area: its mountains, rivers, valleys, and plains.

— 6 —
Alice Eastwood:
Plant Pioneer

by Joyce Ray

April 18, 1906

$\mathcal{A}$lice ran through the San Francisco rubble. The ground wasn't shaking anymore, but fires burned everywhere. Was the Academy still standing? Could she save the valuable plant **specimens**?

Inside, the stone stairs lay crumbled. The iron banister still wound up six floors to the **herbarium**. Alice and a friend crammed their feet between the rungs and inched up. They bundled dried plants and lowered them by string to the ground floor. When flames threatened the building, they fled. Alice and her helper had saved over one thousand plant specimens.

· · · · ᏬᎧ · · · ·

Alice's love of plants began in Canada when she was six. Her mother died and her father left his three children with country relatives. Alice scouted for wild raspberries and partridge berries.

Their father returned, but left again. He sent Alice and her younger sister to a convent school. Alice, age eight, watched the priest's apple tree experiments. She experimented with geranium seeds from her uncle's garden.

When Alice was 14, her father brought her to Denver, Colorado. He did not have a house yet, so Alice worked as a nanny. The family vacationed in the Rocky Mountains. Alice explored carpets of wildflowers, learning about **botany**.

Later, Alice attended school and kept house for her father, sister, and brother. When money was scarce, she left school to work. Once, she tended the school furnace, went to classes and sewed in a shop after school.

Alice graduated from high school at age 20 and returned to teach. There were very few female botanists in the 1800s. But Alice continued to learn about plants.

In the summers, she collected **alpine** flowers on Grays Peak and Pikes Peak. She flattened sunflowers and columbines in a **plant press.** Afterwards, she studied their parts and labeled them. Some plants were type specimens. These are the first plants in a **species** ever collected and described. They added to the knowledge of botany. Alice was the pioneer who discovered them.

Her life changed in 1891 on a trip to California to study plants. She met the plant **curator** at the California Academy of Sciences. Soon Alice was organizing specimens for the Academy's herbarium. In two years, she became the curator herself.

TIDBITS

Alice added over 300,000 plants to the Academy's collection after the earthquake. She named 125 new species of plants growing in California.

• ─ •

Alice found a new member of the sunflower family. Elegant Eastwood or *Eastwoodia elegans* is named after her.

• ─ •

Alice loved lupine flowers. Today they grow along with strawberries and poppies on the roof of the new California Academy of Sciences.

Now, Alice had a job she loved. With a plant press on her back, she hiked or rode a horse, collecting poppies and lupine. Wearing dresses and riding sidesaddle did not work. But women didn't wear pants then. So Alice sewed a split denim skirt with hidden buttons, front and back. She buttoned them while walking. For riding, she opened the flaps and buttoned them together on the sides.

In the 1800s, botanists didn't know much about plants in America's west. Alice became the expert. She hiked fast - up to twenty miles a day. Once she tramped through snow to Mount Shasta's summit. On the way down, she tucked in her corduroy skirt and slid down the volcano!

Alice collected specimens from the Rockies to the Sierras and from Big Sur to the Yukon. She discovered and named unknown plants. Alice kept careful records and traded specimens with others.

Alice Eastwood rescued more than plant specimens after the earthquake. During her life, she rescued wildflowers and redwoods. Alice talked and wrote about protecting the environment. People listened to her. They created parks where everyone could enjoy nature. Alice was a true plant pioneer.

Alice continued her work with plants until she was 90 years old.

Timeline: Alice Eastwood

1859	►	January 19, Alice Eastwood is born in Toronto, Canada to Colin and Eliza Eastwood.
1865	►	Her mother dies.
1867	►	Alice's father moves to Denver, Colorado with her brother. Alice and her sister stay at a convent school in Oshawa, Canada.
1873	►	Alice joins her father in Denver.
1879	►	Graduates first in her class from Denver East High School and becomes a teacher.
1887	►	Guides naturalist Alfred Russel Wallace up Grays Peak in the Rockies in search of alpine flowers. She writes about her trips for *Zoe*, a nature magazine.
1892	►	Becomes joint Curator of Botany at the California Academy of Sciences, under Katherine Brandegee.
1893	►	Becomes Curator and Head of the Department of Botany at California Academy of Sciences and editor of *Zoe*. Publishes *A Popular Flora of Denver, Colorado*.
1903	►	*American Men of Science* lists Alice's name with the star of a top botanist.
1905	►	Publishes *A Handbook of the Trees of California*.
1906	►	San Francisco earthquake destroys California Academy of Sciences.
1906–1912	►	Studies plant collections in Washington, DC, New York, Boston, London and Paris.
1912	►	Returns to California Academy of Sciences as Curator.
1932–1966	►	Publishes a journal, "Leaflets of Western Botany," with John Thomas Howell.
1949	►	Retires as Curator at California Academy of Sciences at age 90 after 57 years.
1950	►	Honorary president of the Seventh International Botanical Congress, Stockholm, Sweden.
1953	►	October 30, dies in San Francisco.

Learn More About Alice Eastwood and Botany

- Burnie, David. *Plant (DK/Google E.guides)*. DK Children. 2006.
- Burns, Diane. *Wildflowers, Blooms & Blossoms (Take-Along Guide)*. Northword Books. 1998.
- Ross, Michael Elsohn and Caple, Laurie A. *Flower Watching With Alice Eastwood.* Carolrhoda Books. 1997.

Web sites:

- Wildflower photos and common and scientific names: http://aggie-horticulture.tamu.edu/wildseed/wildflowers.html
- Name parts of a flower activity: http://www.bbc.co.uk/schools/scienceclips/ages/9_10/life_cycles.shtml
- Learn about the living roof on the new California Academy of Sciences: http://www.calacademy.org/academy/building/the_living_roof.phpl
- Information about Carl Linnaeus and his flower clock: http://www.dimdima.com/Science/science_common/show_science.asp?q_aid = 146&q_title = Carl + Linnaeus

Glossary

alpine (AL pine) Having to do with the upward slope of a mountain, above the timberline—the area where trees can no longer grow.

botany (BOT uh nee) The scientific study of plants.

curator (KYOO ray tur) The person in charge of a museum or an art gallery.

herbarium (ur BAIR ee uhm) A collection of dried plant specimens.

plant press (PLANT PRESS) A gadget that helps preserve the shape and outline of a plant while it is drying. The dried plant can then be displayed.

species (SPEE sheez) One of the groups into which animals and plants of the same genus are divided according to their shared characteristics.

specimen (SPESS uh muhn) A sample or an example used to stand for a whole group such as a butterfly specimen.

— 7 —
Maud Younger:
Millionaire Waitress

by Linda Crotta Brennan

For three days Maud Younger walked the streets of New York looking for a job. She went into every restaurant she saw, and was thrilled when she was finally hired. She washed tables, took orders, and learned how to balance heavy plates on her arm. At the end of the day, she was tired, so tired. But waitresses only earned $4 a week.

"Well, I suppose the tips will help me out," Maud said to another waitress.

"Tips!" The girl laughed and told Maud most waitresses got none.

"Can they live on their wages?" Maud asked.

The girl looked at her. "What did you work at before?"

"I never worked in a restaurant," Maud told her.

"I thought not," the girl said, "or you'd know a girl can't live long on $4 a week."

Maud didn't say that she'd never had a job before. Maud was so wealthy, she didn't need to work. She had stopped in New York on her way to Paris. She planned to visit a **settlement house** for a week and see the **slums**. She ended up staying five years.

· · · · ∾ · · · ·

The College Settlement House of New York, where Maud stayed, was established by women college graduates to help the poor. It was in New York's crowded East Side, the home of many immigrants.

◆—

In 1920, Maud drove her convertible across country from California to Washington D.C., with only her dog for company. This was a dangerous trip in a time before paved roads.

Maud was born in San Francisco in 1870. Her father, William John Younger, was a successful dentist. Her mother, Annie Maria Younger, came from a wealthy family. Maud had one brother and three sisters.

When Maud was twelve, her mother died. She left her children a large fortune. Maud went to private schools and traveled often. Two of her sisters married European royalty. Her father moved to Paris and set up a fashionable dental practice there.

When she was 31, Maud set off to visit her father in Paris. Along the way, she stopped in New York to visit a friend who was staying in a settlement house. The visit changed Maud's life.

She took a job as a waitress to see what it was like to be a working girl. She became active in the Waitresses' **Union**. She wrote about the experience for magazines.

When Maud returned home to San Francisco, she found another waitressing job. This earned her the nickname, "The Millionaire Waitress." She discovered the waitresses in California didn't have a union, so she started one. She helped get the eight hour law passed in California. This law said employers couldn't make women work more than eight hours a day.

Maud also fought for women's **suffrage,** the right to vote. She spoke to lawmakers and organized working women. In a San Francisco parade, she drove a team of six white horses pulling a float for women's rights. California passed a law giving women the right to vote in 1911. At that time, only five other states allowed women full suffrage.

Maud headed back to New York to support women **garment workers** in their **strike**. Then she joined the fight for women's suffrage on a national level. She was the second in command of the National Women's Party. This group **picketed** the White House. Many of the women were arrested. In prison, they went on **hunger strikes**. Maud gave speeches all over the country about what was happening.

Finally, in 1920, the **19th Amendment** to the Constitution passed, granting all women in the United States the right to vote.

Maud went on to fight for the **Equal Rights Amendment**. This amendment would give women equal rights with men. Despite the efforts of Maud and many others, this amendment has never been passed.

Maud died of cancer at the age of sixty six. She's remembered as a fierce fighter for working women and women's rights.

Maud Younger drove her car across the country with only her dog, Sandy, for company.

Timeline: Maud Younger

1870 ➤ January 10, Maud is born in San Francisco to William John Younger and Annie Maria Younger.

1882 ➤ Maud's mother dies.

1900 ➤ Maud's father moves to Paris.

1901–1906 ➤ Maud lives at the College Settlement House in New York City, while working as a waitress.

1907 ➤ Writes about her experience as a waitress for *McClure's Magazine*.

1908 ➤ Returns to San Francisco and forms the San Francisco waitress union

Helps organize Wage Earners' Equal Suffrage League.

1908–1911 ➤ Is a delegate for the San Francisco Central Trades and Labor Council.

1911 ➤ The Eight Hour Work Day Law passes in California. Women win the right to vote in California.

1912 ➤ Joins the "White Goods Strike" of women garment workers in New York. White goods were fabrics such as cotton or linen.

1916 ➤ Delivers the keynote speech at the founding of the National Women's Party.

1913–1920 ➤ Active in the National Women's Party.

1920 ➤ The 19th Amendment passes, granting women in every state the right to vote.

1923–1936 ➤ Works for passage of the Equal Rights Amendment.

1936 ➤ June 25, Maud dies of cancer at the age of 66, at her ranch in Los Gatos, California.

Learn More About Maud Younger, Women's Suffrage, and Labor Unions

- Bartoletti, Susan Campbell. *Kids on Strike!* Houghton Mifflin, 1999.
- Dash, Joan. *We Shall Not Be Moved: The Women's Factory Strike Of 1909.* Scholastic, 1996.
- Landau, Elaine. *Women's Right to Vote.* Children's Press, 2005.

Web site:

- A short biography of Maud Younger:
  http://womenshistory.about.com/library/bio/blbio_younger_maud.htm

Glossary

Equal Rights Amendment (EE kwuhl RITESS uh MEND muhnt) A suggested change to the United States Constitution which was to guarantee equal rights under the law for Americans regardless of sex. The amendment has been suggested in every Congress since 1982, but it has never passed.

garment workers (GAR muhnt WUR kurz) People who make clothing in factories.

hunger strikes (HUHNG uhr STRIKESS) The act of fasting or going without food in order to achieve a particular social change.

19th Amendment (nine TEENTH uh MEND muhnt) The amendment to the United States Constitution which gave women the right to vote.

picket (PIK it) To stand outside a place and protest or try to prevent people from entering a building.

settlement house (SET uhl muhnt HOUSS) Houses set up for the poor to provide shelter, food, and often schooling. Wealthy people sponsored the houses and often volunteered to help.

slums (SLUHMZ) An overcrowded and poor part of a town or city. The homes in a slum area are usually in poor condition.

strike (STRIKE) The act of stopping work in order to force owners and employers to provide better pay, work hours, or other benefits.

suffrage (SUHF rij) The right to vote.

union (YOON yuhn) An organized group of workers set up to help improve working conditions.

— 8 —
Charlotta S. Bass:
Journalist and Activist

by Marty Darragh

Charlotta Bass once said, "I will not retire nor will I retreat, not one inch, so long as God gives me the vision to see what is happening and strength to fight for the things I know are right."

And, that's what she did for forty years through her newspaper.

· · · · ᧓ · · · ·

Charlotta Amanda Spears was born around 1880. Her birthplace was probably Sumter, South Carolina. She was the sixth of eleven children. Her father, Hiram, was a bricklayer. Her mother, Kate, was a housewife.

About 1900, Charlotta moved to Providence, Rhode Island. She worked at the *Providence Watchman* newspaper. For health reasons she moved to Los Angeles, California, in 1910. Charlotta went to work for the *Eagle*, the oldest black newspaper in California. Charlotta earned $5.00 a week selling **subscriptions**.

John J. Neimore had started the *Eagle* in 1879. In 1912 he became very sick. He asked Charlotta to take over as editor. Neimore died soon after.

One year later, Charlotta bought the paper at a public **auction** for $50.00. She changed its name to *California Eagle*.

In 1913, Charlotta hired Joseph Blackburn (J.B.) Bass as Editor. The paper became more political after J.B. arrived. Charlotta and J.B. were good business partners. In 1914, they became life partners when they married.

Charlotta used the paper to fight **discrimination**. Around 1915 she tried to stop the movie *Birth of a Nation*. It showed the **Ku Klux Klan** in very good terms. Blacks were shown **negatively**. Charlotta urged blacks not to work in the film. She sued to have the film stopped but lost.

Next, she took on the Los Angeles fire department. She wrote opinion pieces called editorials. She pointed out that the city had no black fire fighters. After three months, the first black fireman was hired. Charlotta learned there were no black nurses or nurses' aides working at the Los Angeles County Hospital. She set up a kind of employment agency. The County Board of **Supervisors** supported her. Charlotta placed black women in hospital jobs.

In the late 1920s, Charlotta began a front page editorial called "On the Sidewalk." She used the column to change the way blacks were treated in Los Angeles. Charlotta wanted fair employment practices. The paper joined the national campaign of "Don't Shop Where You Can't Work" during the 1930s. She also went up against the Southern California Telephone Company. Over one hundred black families canceled their phone service before blacks were hired in 1936.

TIDBITS

When Charlotta took over the *Eagle*, it had $50 in cash but owed $150.

•◆•

Charlotta sued a restaurant in 1925 for not serving her and her friends.

•◆•

She took journalism classes at Columbia University in NY for three months from 1926-1927.

TIDBITS

Starting in 1938, Charlotta had a news radio program.

•◆•

The FBI had a 563 page file on her when she died.

•◆•

The *Los Angeles Times* did not publish her obituary when she died.

Some neighborhoods in Los Angeles used **covenants** to keep blacks from buying property. Charlotta rallied black professionals. They took the fight to court and won. Charlotta didn't stop until the U.S. Supreme Court ruled the covenants illegal in 1948.

Charlotta spoke out about the differences in the way people of color were treated in America. Because she did so, Charlotta was suspected of being a **Communist**. She was investigated for un-American activities by the FBI. Agents visited the newspaper in 1942.

Charlotta sold the newspaper in 1951. She moved to New York City to work for the Progressive Party. The party asked her to run for Vice President in 1952.

After the campaign she retired to Lake Elsinor, California. Charlotta had a stroke in 1966 and returned to Los Angeles. She died in 1969.

Charlotta Bass and Eagle production staff.

Timeline: Charlotta S. Bass

c1880 ► Charlotta is born in South Carolina. Her parents are Hiram and Kate Spears.

c1900 ► She moves to Providence, Rhode Island.

1910 ► Charlotta moves to Los Angeles. She goes to work at the *Eagle*.

1912 ► She takes over the *Eagle*.

1913 ► Charlotta hires Joseph Blackburn (J.B.) Bass as Editor.

1914 ► J.B. And Charlotta are married.

c1915 ► She tries to stop the filming of the movie *Birth of a Nation*.

1917 ► Charlotta convinces Los Angeles County Hospital to hire black women.

1920s ► Charlotta begins reporting on the Ku Klux Klan.

1925 ► The Klan sues Charlotta and J.B. The Basses win the case.

1930 ► Founds the Industrial Council to fight discrimination and encourage black businesses.

1934 ► J.B. Dies.

1943 ► Charlotta stands up against police brutality targeting Mexican-American youth.

1940s ► She begins to fight for **civil liberties** and is investigated.

1945 ► Charlotta runs for Los Angeles City Council and loses.

1947 ► She joins the Progressive Party. This political party wanted to end segregation, give blacks full voting rights, and find a way to give everyone health insurance.

1948 ► The Supreme Court rules covenants to keep blacks from buying property are illegal.

1951 ► Charlotta sells the *California Eagle* and moves to New York City.

1952 ► She is nominated as the Vice Presidential candidate by the Progressive Party. Charlotta is the first black to run for national office. After losing, she moves to Lake Elsinor, California.

1966 ► Charlotta has a stroke and moves back to Los Angeles.

1969 ► April 29, Charlotta dies.

NOTE : c1880 means about or around 1880

Learn More about Charlotta Bass, Black Women Leaders, and the Newspaper Business

- Craig, Janet and Richard Max Kolding. *What's It Like to Be a Newspaper Reporter (Young Careers)*. Troll Communications LLC, 1990.

- Pinkney, Andrea Davis. *Let It Shine: Stories of Black Women Freedom Fighters*. Gullivar Books, 2000.

- Welch, Catherine A. *Ida B. Wells-Barnett: Powerhouse With a Pen (Trailblazer Biographies)*. Carolrhoda Books, 2000.

Web site:

- More about Charlotta Bass and her work on the *California Eagle*: http://www.socallib.org/bass/story/index.html

Glossary

auction (AWK shuhn) A sale where goods are sold to the person who offers the most money for them.

civil liberties (SIV il LIB ur teez) The freedom from government interference in one's life.

Communists (KOM yuh nistss) A political party that believes the government should own all land, houses, and factories and that profits should be shared by all the citizens.

covenants (KUH vuh nent) A formal agreement.

discrimination (DISS krim i NAY shuhn) Prejudice or unfair treatment of others because of their race, age, religion, etc.

Ku Klux Klan (KOO kluks klan) A terrorist group formed in the United States after the Civil War that is known for targeting African Americans, Jews, Roman Catholics, and others.

negatively (NEG uh tiv lee) Showing someone in a bad light.

subscriptions (sub SKRIP shuhnz) Money paid to receive a newspaper or magazine regularly.

supervisors (SOO pur vye zurz) People who watch and direct the work of others.

Ethel Percy Andrus:
A Life of Service to Others

by Patty Lyman Schremmer

Ethel drove farther and farther outside the city of Los Angeles. She finally found the retired teacher she had heard needed help. The teacher was living in an old chicken coop. It was all she could afford. Ethel knew she would find a way to help this woman. No one should have to live like this!

· · · · ⌒ · · · ·

Ethel Percy Andrus was born in San Francisco in 1884. Her family moved to Chicago when Ethel was young. Ethel grew up in Chicago and graduated from Austin High School.

Very few women went to college in the early 1900s. Ethel did. She graduated from the University of Chicago in 1903. Then she taught English and German at the Lewis Institute.

Ethel thought it was important to serve her community. She volunteered at **settlement houses** in Chicago.

TIDBITS

The students at Lincoln High were from so many backgrounds, they spoke 32 different languages.

•◆•

Ethel believed "we must do some good for which the pay is only the satisfaction of knowing we have provided an important service." Her motto was, "to serve, not be served." That became AARP's motto.

•◆•

Ethel's pension in 1944 was $60 a month.

In 1910 Ethel went back to California with her family. She taught in high schools. In 1916 she became principal of the East Los Angeles High School. She was the first woman high school principal in California.

The East Los Angeles High School had problems. The 2,500 students were mostly from poor families. **Racial and cultural conflicts** divided the students. The school had a high **delinquency** rate.

Ethel had a plan. She wanted the students to feel good about themselves and about the school. She changed the school's name to Abraham Lincoln High School. She thought students would feel better about a school named after such an inspiring president.

Ethel set up a community service project. Students worked as helpers in hospitals, supervised playgrounds, ran a toy-lending library, and much more.

Ethel arranged school assemblies, sports events, and dances for the students. She visited families in their homes.

Ethel's plan worked. The school's delinquency rate dropped. Ethel and the school received awards for the drop in juvenile crime.

Ethel continued her education while working. She got a Masters degree in 1928 and a Ph.D. in 1930. She was called Dr. Andrus.

Dr. Andrus was principal of Lincoln High for 28 years. She retired in 1944. Ethel was 60 years old, but she still had things to do. Her greatest accomplishments came when she

advocated for older people.

Ethel volunteered with the California Retired Teachers Association. She was shocked to learn that most retired teachers had very small **pensions**. Many had no **health insurance** to help pay doctor bills.

Ethel made a plan. No more retired teachers living in chicken coops!

Ethel founded the National Retired Teachers Association (NRTA) in 1947. She worked hard to get better pensions and health insurance for retired educators.

Ethel decided to create a larger group to meet the needs of even more people. She had noticed that many people who retired didn't feel good about themselves without a purpose in their days. Ethel knew that older people, just like her high school students, needed to keep helping others.

In 1958 she established the American Association of Retired Persons (AARP). Until her death, Ethel worked tirelessly to promote the understanding of aging and to improve life for all older people.

Ethel died in 1967, at age 82.

AARP is over 50 years old and has more than 39 million members. The organization still operates on Ethel Percy Andrus's original plan: to promote independence, dignity, and purpose for all older Americans.

TIDBITS

In 1960, Ethel supervised the creation of the "House of Freedom." She was a pioneer in adapting house designs to meet the needs of older people. Adaptations included such things as stepless entries, lever door handles (rather than round knobs, which can be hard for older people to grip and turn), and faucets that push and pull. This concept later became known as "Universal Design."

President Eisenhower looks over AARP's scale model of the House of Freedom in Washington, D.C. in 1961.

Timeline: Ethel Percy Andrus

1884 ➤ September 21, Ethel Percy Andrus is born to George Wallace Andrus and his wife, Lucretia Frances Duke. She is the younger of two daughters.

1885 ➤ The Andrus family moves to Chicago.

1903 ➤ Ethel graduates from the University of Chicago.

1910 ➤ The family moves back to California.

1916 ➤ Ethel becomes principal of the East Lost Angeles High School. She renames it the Abraham Lincoln High School.

1928 ➤ She receives a Masters Degree from the University of Southern California, Los Angeles.

1930 ➤ She receives a Ph.D., also from USC.

1944 ➤ Ethel retires to care for her elderly mother. She soon becomes volunteer Director of Welfare for the California Retired Teachers Association.

1947 ➤ Ethel founds the National Retired Teachers Association to give retired teachers a stronger, nation-wide voice. She is the NRTA's first president.

1950 ➤ She launches the *NRTA Journal*, which she edits.

1954 ➤ She brings to reality Grey Gables, the first and only national teachers' retirement home, in Ojai, California.

Dr. Andrus is the first teacher to receive the Golden Apple Award, when she is named Teacher of the Year on Teacher Remembrance Day.

1958 ➤ Ethel establishes the American Association of Retired Persons, becomes its first President, founds and edits its magazine, *Modern Maturity*.

1960 ➤ Ethel conceives and supervises the development of the House of Freedom, designed to make living easier for older people. President Eisenhower appoints her to the National Advisory Committee for the 1961 White House Conference on Aging.

1964 ➤ The Ethel Percy Andrus **Gerontology** Center is established at USC in Los Angeles, for training and research in human development and aging.

1967 ➤ July 13, Ethel Percy Andrus dies in Long Beach, CA.

Learn More About Ethel Percy Andrus and Related Topics

- Crippen, Dorothy, et al. **Power of Years: The Wisdom of Ethel Percy Andrus.** National Retired Teachers Association and American Association of Retired Persons, 1968. (biography, pp. 9-12)

- Higgins, Ardis O. **Windows on Women.** Halls of Ivy Press, 1975. (profile, pp. 49-50 This book has an extensive listing of resource materials about numerous women throughout history.)

Web sites:

- Biography of Ethel Percy Andrus:
  http://assets.aarp.org/www.aarp.org_/articles/NRTA/andrus_bio.pdf

- American Association of Retired Persons (AARP):
  http://www.aarp.org/

- Universal Design:
  http://www.design.ncsu.edu/cud

Glossary

advocated (AD vuh kay tuhd) Supported or worked for another person's ideas or rights.

delinquency (di LING kwuhnt see) Repeated trouble with the police.

gerontology (jer uhn TAW luh jee) The scientific study of the problems of aging.

health insurance (HELTH in SHU ruhnss) Regular payments to a company that agrees to pay your medical bills in the event of sickness or accident.

pensions (PEN shuhnz) An amount of money paid each month to a person who has retired from work.

racial and cultural conflicts (RAY shuhl and kuhl chur uhl KON flictss) Serious disagreements that occur because of the differences in the ways people of different races or income levels might live or because of different group traditions.

settlement houses (SET uhl muhnt HOUSS uhz) Houses set up for the poor to provide shelter, food, and often schooling. Wealthy people sponsored the houses and often volunteered to help.

— 10 —
Ruth Law:
Daring Aviator

by Janet Buell

The shining city of Washington, D.C. stretched below Ruth Law. She pushed the control. The little wood and **canvas** aeroplane nosed lower.

Ruth could see people staring up. For some, this was their first glimpse of a plane. Few could know its pilot was a woman.

The target was almost below her. Ruth moved the **lever**. She felt the pressure of the turn. Ruth was flying upside down over the White House.

· · · · Ꮿ · · · ·

Ruth Law was born on March 21, 1887 in Lynn, Massachusetts. Ruth and her brother Rodman were daredevil children. Their mother told people she felt like a hen who'd hatched two ducklings.

As a young adult, Ruth watched men at a nearby flight school. Ruth convinced one to take her up. Ruth knew then she'd some day fly her own plane. It was a time when most women didn't even drive cars.

Flight instructors refused to teach Ruth. Eventually, one agreed. Ruth got her pilot's license. She flew in exhibitions and got paid for them.

In early November 1916, Victor Carlstrom flew 452 miles nonstop from Chicago to New York State. It was an American distance record.

Ruth decided she could best him. Ruth tried to borrow a plane like Carlstrom's. The manufacturer refused. He didn't think women were strong enough to fly bigger planes.

Carlstrom had flown in an enclosed cockpit. Ruth's seat was open to the wind. A windshield fitted to her plane would help protect her. She could not hold a map. Ruth needed her hands to operate the levers. She designed a map holder that strapped to her knee. Mechanics also outfitted her little plane with an extra fuel tank.

A fierce wind blew the day Ruth took off from Chicago. The little plane pitched and shook. A mechanic cried as she finally gained altitude. He thought Ruth would crash.

Over Ohio, Ruth encountered snow. It was bitterly cold. She landed in Hornell, NY – a distance of 590 miles. Ruth beat Carlstrom by 138 miles.

During World War I, Ruth flew her plane for the war effort. She dropped paper "bombs" across America. These **leaflets** asked people to donate money. Ruth also believed women pilots could help. Congress considered a bill that would allow women to fly supply missions. Ruth **lobbied** her congressmen. She flew upside down over the White House, and landed on Pennsylvania

TIDBITS

Ruth learned to fly by grass mowing – driving the plane up and down a grassy landing strip. One day, Ruth got the plane airborne. She wasn't ready for that step. Ruth had trouble flying right side up. 500 feet up, she realized she didn't know how to land. People watched anxiously. Ruth pulled herself together and figured it out. Later she told people it was by sheer luck she got back safely.

Avenue. Despite her exhibits, the bill didn't pass.

After the war, Ruth organized Ruth Law's Flying Circus. The public wanted to see dangerous stunts. Ruth raced her plane against cars. She dropped from a rope ladder into a moving car. She walked the wings. Ruth stood harnessed to the top of the plane while the pilot pushed it into three loop the loops.

Ruth had been at the wheel of a car when a young stunt woman died in October 1921. A ladder hung from an airplane that flew low overhead as the car raced along. The young woman stood in the car. She caught the ladder to climb into the airplane, but lost her grip. She fell to the pavement and fractured her skull.

Not long after, in March of 1922, Ruth retired from flying. She and her husband, Charles, moved to Beverly Hills. Here, Ruth got to meet and mingle with Hollywood celebrities. They eventually settled in San Francisco. Ruth died there on December 2, 1970 at age eighty-three.

Ruth Law's Flying Circus

Timeline: Ruth Law

1887	➤	March 21, Ruth Bancroft Law is born in Lynn, MA.
1903	➤	December 17, the Wright Brothers fly the world's first successful airplane.
1910	➤	Ruth marries Charles Oliver.
1912	➤	Enrolls in Burgess Flying School in Boston. She takes both air and **shop** lessons, where she learns to dismantle and reconstruct airplane engines.
		July 1 -- Harriet Quimby falls to her death during an exhibition near Boston, MA. Ruth and hundreds of others watch. It's the first day of Ruth's flying lessons.
		August 1, flies solo for the first time.
		September, Ruth makes her first exhibition flight. After the show, thousands of spectators rush the field to catch a glimpse of the lady flier.
		November, receives her pilot's license.
1913	➤	Moves to Florida with Charles. A hotel employs her to fly their guests.
1914–1916	➤	Continues flying at air fairs and other events across the country.
1916	➤	November 19, breaks three nonstop cross-country records.
		December 2, Ruth flies over the Statue of Liberty as it's lit for the first time.
1917	➤	April 6, U.S. enters World War I.
		Ruth flies for the war effort, dropping paper "bombs" across America. December, a bill is introduced to Congress to allow women to fly for the military.
		Sets a women's altitude record, flying to 14,700 feet during a war bond exhibition. It takes her one and a half hours to fly to that height.
1918–1922	➤	Ruth and Charles tour Europe, Philippines, China, Japan. Ruth starts her Flying Circus.
1921	➤	Ruth is at the wheel of a car during a stunt that kills a young woman.
1922	➤	Charles Oliver releases the news that Ruth is retiring from flying.
1970	➤	December 2 -- Ruth dies at age 83. She's buried in Lynn, Massachusetts.

Learn More About Ruth Law and Early Days of Flying

- Bledsoe, Karen E. *Daredevils of the Air: Thrilling Tales of Pioneer Aviators.* Avisson Press, Inc., 2003.

- Brown, Don. *Ruth Law Thrills A Nation.* Sandpiper, 1995.

- Langley, Wanda. *Women of the Wind: Early Women Aviators.* Morgan Reynolds Publishing, 2006.

Web sites:

- A short biography of Ruth Law:
  http://www.hill.af.mil/library/factsheets/factsheet.asp?id = 5877

- Pictures and stories about Ruth Law:
  http://www.ctie.monash.edu.au/hargrave/law.html

Glossary

canvas (KAN vuhss) A type of rough, strong cloth often used for making sails or tents.

leaflets (LEEF letss) Single sheets of paper or small posters that give information.

lever (LEV ur) A bar or handle used to work or control a machine.

lobbied (LOB eed) Worked to convince politicians to vote a certain way.

shop (SHOP) The name given to a class in high school or elsewhere that teaches students about mechanics, carpentry, and other skills.

—11—
Dorothea Lange: Changing the World through Photography

by Linda Crotta Brennan

Dorothea Lange ran a well-known portrait studio in San Francisco. She took photographs of wealthy and famous people. But trouble was brewing.

The **stock market crashed** on October 24, 1929. Businesses closed. Men were thrown out of work. Families were penniless.

Jobless men drifted through streets outside Dorothea's studio. She felt driven to record what was happening. Easing through the crowds, she reached a line waiting for handouts from a **soup kitchen**. Quietly, she set up her camera. She began snapping shots of weary men eating from battered plates and tin cups.

She hung the photographs in her studio. "What are you going to do with this kind of thing?" one of her wealthy customers asked. Dorothea didn't know, but she sensed this kind of photography was worth doing.

· · · · ᎧᏅ · · · ·

Dorothea understood trouble. She was born Dorothea Nutzhorn in Hoboken, NJ, on May 25, 1895. When she was seven, she came down with **polio.** The disease crippled her right leg. She limped for the rest of her life.

When Dorothea was twelve, her father deserted the family. She and her mother and brother were forced to move in with her grandmother. Dorothea's mother went to work at the New York Public Library. She took Dorothea to school in New York. Dorothea hated school, but she loved the picture collections at her mother's library. And as she walked the streets of New York, she studied the faces of poor **immigrants.**

When she graduated, Dorothea decided she wanted to be a photographer, even though she'd never taken a picture. She found part-time jobs working for photographers, some of them very well-known. They taught her the skills she needed.

At twenty-two, Dorothea and a friend headed west. They ended up in San Francisco. Dorothea never forgave her father for leaving her family. So she dropped her father's name, taking her mother's maiden name instead. As Dorothea Lange, she opened her own photography studio.

She attracted many rich clients. In the evenings, artists and writers would gather in her studio to talk and drink tea. One was the western painter, Maynard Dixon. Although he was 20 years older than Dorothea, they fell in love and married.

They had two sons, Daniel and John, but their marriage was troubled. Maynard often took off into the wilderness to paint— for months at a time.

Then the stock market fell. An economics professor named Paul Taylor saw Dorothea's haunting photographs of the soup kitchen. He contacted her and asked if she would provide photographs to go with his report on the **Great Depression**. Dorothea agreed.

Working closely together, Dorothea and Paul fell in love. In 1935 Dorothea divorced Maynard Dixon and married Paul Taylor.

Paul and Dorothea documented the difficult lives of **migrant farm workers**. Some of Dorothea's most famous photographs come from this time period, particularly "The Migrant Mother."

The Migrant Mother

Japanese American internees

On December 7, 1941, Japan bombed Pearl Harbor. The United States was thrown into World War II. Fearing that Japanese immigrants might aid the enemy, the government sent them to live in **Internment Camps**. Dorothea photographed these Japanese families as they were led away from their homes.

Dorothea continued to work until she died at the age of 70. A pioneer in **documentary photography**, she recorded the lives of common people across the United States and the world.

Timeline: Dorothea Lange

1895 ➤	May 25, Dorothea Margaretta Nutzhorn is born to Henry Nutzhorn and Joanna (Lange) Nutzhorn in Hoboken, NJ. She is their first child.
1901 ➤	Brother, Henry Martin Nutzhorn, is born.
1902 ➤	Becomes ill with polio, which cripples her right leg. She limps for the rest of her life.
1907 ➤	Father, Henry Nutzhorn, abandons his family. Dorothea, and her mother and brother move in with grandmother, Sophia Lange.
1913 ➤	Graduates high school. Mother insists that she start training as a teacher.
1914 ➤	Works nights and weekends in photography studio of the famous photographer, Arnold Genthe, in New York.
1918 ➤	Moves to San Francisco. Changes name from Dorothea Nutzhorn to Dorothea Lange.
1919 ➤	Opens own studio.
1920 ➤	March 21, marries Maynard Dixon.
1925 ➤	May 15, son Daniel Dixon born.
1928 ➤	June 12, son John Dixon born.
1929 ➤	October 24, the Stock Market crashes.
1933 ➤	Takes photos of the soup kitchen: "White Angel Bread Line."
1934 ➤	Paul Taylor asks her to do photographs for his report on the Great Depression.
1935 ➤	Joins Paul Taylor in doing field work for the government.
	November, divorces Maynard Dixon.
	December 6, marries Paul Taylor.
1936–1939 ➤	Photographs workers, farmers, and the unemployed across the United States.
1941 ➤	December 7, the Japanese bomb Pearl Harbor. The US enters World War II.
1942 ➤	Photographs the internment of Japanese-Americans.
1958–1959 ➤	Travels with husband to Asia, South America, Africa, and Europe.
1965 ➤	Organizes show of her photographs for Museum of Modern Art in New York.
1965 ➤	October 11, dies in California of throat cancer.

Learn More About Dorothea Lange and Photography

- Bidner, Jenni. ***The Kid's Guide to Digital Photography.*** Lark Books, 2004.

- Meltzer Milton. ***Dorothea Lange: Life Through The Camera.*** Viking Kestrel, 1985.

- Partridge, Elizabeth. ***Restless Spirit: The Life and Work of Dorothea Lange.*** Viking, 1998.

Web site:

- Dorothea Lange online collections, Oakland Museum of California
  http://www.museumca.org/global/art/collections_dorothea_lange.html

---

Glossary

documentary photography (dok yuh MEN tuh ree fuh TOG ruh fee) A series of pictures that tell a story about real people or events.

Great Depression (GRAYT di PRESH uhn) The period from 1929 to 1940 when many American businesses did badly and people became poor.

immigrants (IM uh gruhntss) People who come from abroad to live permanently in another country.

internment camps (in TUHRN ment KAMPSS) Also called War Relocation Camps. Places where thousands of Japanese Americans were forced to live during World War II because many people feared Japanese living in America would help the country of Japan. The families were forced to leave their homes and businesses.

migrant farm worker (MYE gruhnt FARM WUR kur) A person who moves from farm to farm helping with seasonal work.

polio (POH lee oh) A disease that attacks the brain and spinal chord. It occurred mainly in children and often caused paralysis. Today, this disease is easily prevented with a vaccine.

soup kitchen (SOOP KICH uhn) A place that feeds meals to the poor and homeless.

Stock Market Crash (STOK MAR kit KRASH) October 29, 1929, also called "Black Tuesday." Thousands of investors tried to sell their shares in companies. The result was that companies failed and people lost their jobs. The Stock Market Crash is known as the beginning of the Great Depression.

—12—
Mabel Fairbanks:
Skater Breaks the Ice Barrier

by Deborah Bruss

Mabel Fairbanks gazed at the ice skates in the **pawnshop** window. She opened her hand and counted her money one more time. She still did not have enough.

She closed her eyes and imagined herself gliding across the ice. She wanted to skate just like the people in Central Park. Mabel took a deep breath and opened the door to the pawnshop. Maybe the owner would sell them for less.

A few minutes later she came out clutching the skates. She twirled on the sidewalk and ran home.

The skates were too big so she stuffed the toes with cotton. Then she headed to a patch of frozen water in Harlem. A stranger watched her try to skate. He told her to go to Central Park where the ice was smooth.

At the park people looked at her as she laced up her skates. They stared at her when she stepped onto the ice. They whispered about her while she taught herself to push and glide.

· · · · ☙ · · · ·

Many years later, Mabel recalled the first time she skated in Central Park. "Blacks didn't skate there. But it was a public place, so I carried on." Mabel never quit skating, even when **discrimination** blocked her way.

Mabel was born in Florida. After her mother died she moved to New York City. Not much is known about her childhood because Mabel did not like to talk about it. Mabel taught herself the basics of figure skating by watching others in Central Park. When the ice melted, she tried an indoor rink. The **cashier** would not let her in. She kept trying until a kind manager said she could practice in the early morning before the rink opened. She began to teach herself spins and jumps.

Some professional skaters watched. They were amazed by her talent and gave her free lessons. Mabel hoped to skate in the Olympics but never got the chance because of her skin color. That fact did not stop her from doing what she loved best. Mabel performed in Harlem for mostly black audiences. She also skated in small ice shows at New York social clubs. She wasn't allowed to be a part of the all-white cast so they called her an "extra added **attraction**."

In 1940 she moved to southern California. For the next ten years she skated in traveling ice shows. **Audiences** in Mexico and South America did not judge her by her color. When she returned to her home she went to Pasadena Winter Gardens. They would not let her in. "But it was a public place," she said, "…so my uncle had newspaper articles written about it and passed them out … until they finally let me in."

TIDBITS

Some reports say that after Mabel moved to New York City, her brother's wife kicked her out and she became homeless until a wealthy woman hired her as a babysitter.

⋅—⋅

Maribel Vinson, who won nine U.S. Championships and three Olympic medals saw Mabel skate in New York. Maribel was so amazed that she gave Mabel free lessons.

⋅—⋅

Mabel sometimes performed on a portable rink. It was only 6 x 6 feet.

TIDBITS

Olympic skaters
Tai Babilonia,
Randy Gardner,
Scott Hamilton,
Kristi Yamaguchi,
and Debi Thomas
were coached by
Mabel.

One of Mabel's
students,
Atoy Wilson,
nominated
Mabel to the U.S.
Figure Skating
Hall of Fame. He
said, "...without
her...I never
would have had
the opportunity
of becoming the
first African
American to
win a U.S.
national title...."

Mabel shared her love of skating for many years. She taught skating to the families of Hollywood stars and gave free lessons to kids who couldn't pay for them. She also coached many talented skaters who went to the Olympics and won National and International Competitions.

Even though Mabel never got the chance to compete, she was not **bitter** about her past. "If I had been allowed," she said, "to go in to the Olympics or Ice Capades like I wanted to then, I may not have helped other blacks... and coached such wonderful skaters... I think all that has been just as important and meaningful."

Mabel Fairbanks (left) rehearses with skating star Mae Edwards. They would perform on the TV show "Frosty Frolics."

Timeline: Mabel Fairbanks

c1915 ➤	Mabel is born in the Florida, though some reports say New York City.
c1923 ➤	Mabel's mother dies and she goes to live with a teacher.
c1924 ➤	Mabel moves to New York City to live with her brother. Mabel watches skaters and falls in love with the sport.
c1926 ➤	Mabel buys her first pair of skates at a pawnshop.
1930's ➤	Ice rinks in New York City refuse to admit Mabel. Finally one lets her in. Maribel Vinson, who won nine U.S. Championships and three Olympic medals, gives Mabel free lessons. Mabel makes a living by skating at nightclubs.
1936 ➤	Mabel wants to try out for the Olympics. First she must join a professional skating club, but these clubs do not allow blacks.
1940 ➤	Mabel moves to Los Angeles. For the next several years she performs in ice shows in countries where black skaters are more accepted.
1943 ➤	*Time Magazine,* in the article, "Swanee Snow Bird," says, "… experts rate her (skating) superior to most white amateurs." Unfortunately, there are several errors in the article, including how old Mabel was.
1940s–1960s ➤	Mabel gives free lessons to children who cannot pay. She teaches Hollywood stars and their families. She becomes well known as a coach. Many of her talented students go on to win World Championships and Olympic medals.
1965 ➤	Mabel fights hard until LA's Culver City skating club becomes the first in the U.S. to admit an African-American.
1966 ➤	Atoy Wilson, coached by Mabel, wins the U.S. Novice Men's division title to become the first African-American national champion.
1995 ➤	Mabel is **diagnosed** with Myasthenia Gravis, a disease that weakens muscles. She continues to coach, but not on the ice.
1997 ➤	She becomes the first black inducted into the U.S. Figure Skating Hall of Fame.
2001 ➤	Mabel Fairbanks dies at age 85 in Los Angeles.

NOTE: c1915 means about or around 1915

Learn More About Mabel Fairbanks and Ice Skating

- Samuels, Rikki. *Kids' Book Of Figure Skating: Skills, Strategies, and Techniques*. Citadel, 2004.

- Schwartz, Heather. *Girls' Figure Skating: Ruling the Rink.* Capstone, 2007.

Web sites:

- Official site of the World Skating Museum and Hall of Fame: http://www.worldskatingmuseum.org/

- Mabel Fairbanks - African American Figure Skater and Ice Skating Coach by Jo Ann Schneider Farris: http://figureskating.about.com/od/famousskaters/p/mabel.htm

Glossary

attraction (uh TRAK shuhn) Something that creates interest, or draws people in.

audiences (AW dee uhnss ez) The people who watch or listen to a performance, speech, or movie.

bitter (BIT ur) Feeling upset or angry about something.

cashier (ka SHIHR) Someone who takes in or pays out money in a store or bank.

diagnosed (dye uhg NOHSST) Found to have a certain disease.

discrimination (diss krim i NAY shuhn) Prejudice or unjust behavior to others based on differences in age, race, or gender.

pawnshop (PAWN shop) A place where people get loans for items they leave as security. If the loan is not repaid, the shop owner may sell the item.

— 13 —
Betty Ford:
First Lady of the United States

by Marty Darragh

$\mathcal{W}$hen Betty Ford was a child, a fortune teller told her she would meet kings and queens. Little did she know the fortune teller was right!

· · · · ໑໑ · · · ·

Elizabeth Ann Bloomer was born in Chicago on April 8, 1918. Her father, William, was a salesman. Betty's mother, Hortense, was a homemaker.

Betty was a tomboy. She wanted to play her older brothers' games. Her mother found a different outlet for Betty's energy. Betty started dancing lessons when she was eight. She took lessons every day. After graduating from high school Betty spent two summers at Bennington School of Dance in Vermont. She studied with the famous dancer, Martha Graham.

At twenty, Betty went to New York City. She wanted more dance study with Martha Graham. Unfortunately, Betty was not good enough to make the primary **troupe** of dancers. She returned home.

In 1942, she married Bill Warren. Betty soon realized the marriage was a mistake. The couple divorced in 1947. That same year, a friend introduced her to Gerald R. (Jerry) Ford. Six months later, Jerry asked Betty to marry him. The wedding, however, could not take place until the fall of 1948. Jerry was running for Congress.

Jerry won the election. The newlyweds went to Washington, D.C. Betty had no idea what Congressmen did. She researched Jerry's job and went to sessions of Congress to watch the debates.

Soon Jerry and Betty started a family. By 1957, they had four children. Because of his job, Jerry was seldom home. Betty was responsible for everything. In 1964 she badly strained her neck. Her doctors gave her painkillers. With Jerry gone so much, Betty became lonely. She started to see a **psychiatrist**. Betty needed someone to talk to. She learned she needed to take care of herself so she could take care of her family.

Betty finally told Jerry about her troubles. Jerry agreed to leave politics at the end of his term in 1974. Then, their lives took a sudden turn. In 1973, Vice President Spiro Agnew resigned. President Richard Nixon appointed Jerry to take his place.

President Nixon had his own problems. He was facing **impeachment** for his part in the **Watergate Scandal** of 1972. Nixon was forced to resign. Betty, who had expected to retire from politics, found herself First Lady.

She decided being First Lady did not mean she had to change who she was inside. Betty was open and honest. When she learned she had breast cancer, she talked openly about her treatment. Betty stressed the importance of early **detection** and millions of women scheduled breast examinations. Betty was an

advocate for women's rights. She used her position to lobby for passage of the **ERA**.

Jerry lost his bid to be elected President in his own right in 1976. Betty and Jerry retired to Palm Springs, California. Jerry, however, was gone as much as before. She was alone again. The children were grown. No one needed her.

Betty continued taking painkillers and other drugs. She also drank too much alcohol. Betty became an addict and an alcoholic. With her family's help, Betty admitted she had a problem and entered a hospital for **rehabilitation**.

Many people realized that if she could admit her problem, they could, too.

Betty wanted to help others. She raised money to open the Betty Ford Center in Rancho Mirage, California. The center provides treatment for alcohol and drug dependency. Betty was actively involved in its day-to-day operations until she was in her eighties.

Betty Ford will be remembered for her courage in facing difficulties and her openness in discussing them.

President Jerry Ford, Betty Ford, and their Golden Retriever, Liberty, in front of the White House

TIDBITS

In Beijing, China, Betty took off her shoes and joined the students at a dancing school.

••

Her daughter, Susan had a sleepover at the White House. The girls slept in the Lincoln Bedroom. Betty put on a white sheet, went into the bedroom, and recited the Gettysburg Address.

••

She read Jerry's **concession** speech after he lost the 1976 presidential election. Jerry had lost his voice.

Time Line: Elizabeth Ann (Betty) Bloomer Ford

1918 ➤ April 8, Betty is born in Chicago, IL to William (Bill) Stephenson and Hortense Neahr Bloomer. She has two older brothers, Bill, Jr. and Bob.

1920 ➤ The Bloomers move to Grand Rapids, Michigan.

1928 ➤ Betty begins dancing lessons.

1936 ➤ She graduates from Central High School.

1938 ➤ She moves to New York City to study dance with Martha Graham.

1941 ➤ Betty returns to Grand Rapids.

1942 ➤ April 23, she marries Bill Warren.

1947 ➤ Betty and Bill Warren divorce.

1948 ➤ October 15, marries Gerald R. (Jerry) Ford.

Jerry is elected to his first term in Congress.

1950–1957 ➤ Four children are born: Michael Gerald, John Gardner—Jack, Steven Meigs, Susan Elizabeth.

1964 ➤ Betty suffers a strained neck and begins taking painkillers.

1973 ➤ December 6, Jerry Ford is named Vice President.

1974 ➤ August 9, Betty becomes First Lady of the United States after Jerry is inaugurated.

September 26, she is diagnosed with breast cancer.

1976 ➤ Gerald Ford loses the presidential election to Jimmy Carter.

1977 ➤ The Fords move to Palm Springs, California.

1978 ➤ Betty checks herself into the Long Beach Naval Hospital's Alcohol and Drug Service. She stays for four weeks.

1982 ➤ October 3, the Betty Ford Center is dedicated.

1987 ➤ She has quadruple heart bypass surgery and almost dies.

1991 ➤ President George H. W. Bush awards Betty the Presidential Medal of Freedom.

1999 ➤ Betty and Jerry receive the Congressional Gold Medal from President Bill Clinton.

2006 ➤ December 26, President Gerald Ford dies.

Learn More About Betty and Jerry Ford

- Bausum, Ann. *Our Country's Presidents: Completely Revised and Expanded.* National Geographic Children's Books, 2005.
- Mattern, Joanne. *Betty Ford.* ABDO Publishing Company, 2008.
- Waxman, Laura Hamilton. *Gerald R. Ford.* Lerner Publications, 2008.

Web sites:

- Gerald R. Ford Presidential Library & Museum: http://fordlibrarymuseum.gov.
- The Betty Ford Center: http://bettyfordcenter.org.

Glossary

advocate (ad vuh KIT) A person who supports an idea or a plan.

concession (kuhn SESH uhn) A speech given by a losing candidate for political office. In a concession speech the candidate admits that the rival party has won the election.

detection (di TEK shuhn) Discovery of the existence of something.

E.R.A. Abbreviation for the Equal Rights Amendment. This proposed change to the United States Constitution would guarantee equal rights to anyone regardless of their gender.

impeachment (im PEECH muhnt) Formal charges brought against a public official who may have committed a crime while in office.

psychiatrist (sye KYE uh trist) A medical doctor who treats mental illnesses.

rehabilitation (ree uh bil uh TAY shuhn) The process of bringing someone back to health.

troupe (TROOP) A dance or theater group.

Watergate Scandal (WAW tur gayt SKAN duhl) A series of crimes approved by President Richard Nixon and members of his staff. The crimes included the theft of documents from the Democratic headquarters at the Watergate Hotel and Offices in Washington, D.C.

—14—

Tsuyako "Sox" Kitashima:
Righting the Wrongs for Japanese Americans

by Deborah Bruss

August, 1981

"Sox" Kitashima listened while many speakers told their stories. They had lost their businesses. Military police had **terrorized** their children. Families had lived behind barbed wire. The more she listened, the more she wanted to make things right.

Finally it was her turn to speak. Her family had been treated like the enemy. They gave up their home and had to live in a horse stall, which still had manure on the floor.

These things happened during World War II. Thousands of people, even American citizens, lost their rights and freedom. These rights should have been protected under the **U.S. Constitution.**

· · · · ❧ · · · ·

Tsuyako Kataoka was born in 1918 near San Francisco. Her parents were *Issei* (Ee-sah), the name given to people who were born in Japan.

72

Issei could not become American citizens. Their children were called *Nisei* (Nee-sah). Since Nisei were born in the U.S., they were citizens. Sox's parents raised six children on their farm.

When Sox was 23, Japan bombed Pearl Harbor and the U.S. entered World War II. Suddenly Sox's life changed.

Japanese Americans were worried because they looked like the enemy. They tried to prove their **loyalty**. They marched with American flags. They destroyed family treasures and photos. Still, they were fired from jobs and barred from restaurants. Nisei tried to join the U.S. military but were turned away.

Anger towards Japanese Americans spread. In 1942, the U.S. military got permission to relocate 120,000 Japanese Americans away from the West Coast.

Sox's family lived in a horse stall at Tanforan Racetrack in California for four months. Then they rode a crowded dirty train for three days. Sox feared they were being sent to die. They arrived at an **internment** camp in Topaz, Utah. Sox and her family lived there for almost four years.

Sox married Tom Kitashima in 1945. Four days later, Japan surrendered. When the newlyweds left Topaz, they were given $50. They went to San Francisco and slept at a **Buddhist** Temple. They found jobs with an agency that was shutting down the camps. The agency also had stored furniture and other things for Japanese Americans. Sadly, most of it had been stolen or ruined. The government did nothing.

Later, Sox worked for the **Veterans' Administration**. She

TIDBITS

When Tsuyako was young, her non-Japanese friends could not say the "Tsu" part of her name. She took on a few nicknames. "Sox" finally stuck.

⋯

Many families were given only 48 hours to pack for the internment camps. Each person was allowed two suitcases. Possessions were put in storage or sold for very little money. One family's beautiful piano sold for $5.

TIDBITS

At the Topaz camp families were given one room, a coal burning stove and one hanging light. Summer temperatures reached 100 degrees; winter nights were often below zero. Fierce dust storms blew sand through building cracks.

•–•

Japanese Americans ran their camps like towns. They built schools, hospitals, farms, and newspapers. Sox worked as a secretary and assistant block manager.

and Tom had one son. Tom died in 1975. Sox kept busy by volunteering for Japanese American causes.

Sox grew up in a culture where men made the decisions and women accepted them. At age 61, Sox decided to speak out. She joined the **National Coalition for Redress and Reparations** (NCRR). Sox got thousands of people to sign letters. She went to Washington, D.C. many times to talk to **Congress**. After seven years of hard work, Congress passed the **Civil Liberties** Act of 1988. Each internee would get $20,000 and an apology.

Sox would not rest until every person got what was promised. Often the apology meant more than the money. For ten years she tracked down people who were homeless, in hospitals, or had left the country. Sadly, by this time, many of the internees had already died. They would never know the U.S. government finally had apologized.

Sox visited many schools and told her story. **"...we must** remember what our Constitution stands for... so that no group will ever experience what we did."

Sox Kitashima speaks to a group. Each candle below her represents one of the World War II internment camps.

Timeline: Tsuyako "Sox" Kitashima

1918 ➤ July 14, Tsuyako is born in Hayward, CA, to Masajiro and Yumi Kataoka.

1936 ➤ Sox graduates from high school, but stays to work on the farm. She also volunteers for Japanese American organizations.

1941 ➤ December 7, Japan bombs Pearl Harbor. Police and the FBI begin to arrest Japanese American leaders without any proof that they are aiding the enemy.

1942 ➤ February 19, President Roosevelt signs Executive Order 9066. It gives the military permission to remove Japanese Americans from the West Coast.

May 9, Sox and her family leave their farm after selling most of their possessions. They go to the Tanforan horse race track, in San Bruno. It is surrounded by barbed wire and armed guards. Four months later they go to a camp in Topaz, Utah, where they live in wooden barracks.

1942–1945 ➤ 120,000 internees live in ten internment camps.

1943–1945 ➤ 33,000 Nisei serve in the US military. Many of them die while fighting on the front lines in Europe and the South Pacific.

1945 ➤ Sox marries Tom Kitashima. August 15, Japan surrenders. By the end of the year, all but one camp closes.

1945–1970 ➤ Japanese Americans quietly struggle to rebuild their lives.

1949 ➤ Sox and Tom have a son, Alan.

1970s ➤ Some Nisei and their children want justice. They begin to educate the public and collect thousands of signatures. Politicians start to listen.

1975 ➤ Sox's husband dies.

1981 ➤ The government forms the CWRIC (Commission on Wartime Relocation and Internment of Civilians). Sox and 750 others testify to the commission.

1983 ➤ The CWRIC recommends that the government give each living internee $20,000.

1988 ➤ The Civil Liberties Act of 1988 grants a formal apology and approves payments to the Japanese Americans.

1989–1999 ➤ Those who had been locked up are paid and given an official apology.

2005 ➤ Sox dies at a nursing home, probably of a heart attack.

Learn More About Sox Katashima and the Interment of Japanese Americans

- Cooper, Michael L. *Remembering Manzanar: Life in a Japanese Relocation Camp.* Clarion Books, 2002.

- Stanley, Jerry. *I am an American: A True Story of Japanese Internment.* Crown Books for Young Readers, 1996.

- Tunnell, Michael O. *The Children of Topaz: The Story of a Japanese American Internment Camp; Based on a Classroom Diary.* Holiday House, 1996.

- Welch, Catherine A. *Children of the Relocation Camps.* Carolrhoda, 2000.

Web sites:

- Sox Kitashima: Dedicated NCRR Volunteer (Video of Sox): http://www.youtube.com/watch?v = fHchGFn81Os

- Japanese-American Internment Montage (story in rap): http://www.youtube.com/watch?v = gTomqDucKnA&feature = related

Glossary

Buddhist (BOO dist) A person who follows the teaching of Buddha and the religion of Buddhism. Buddha was a holy man from India.

civil liberties (SIV il LIB er teez) The freedom from government interference.

Congress (KONG griss) The governing body of the United States, made up of the Senate and the House of Representatives.

internment (in TURN muhnt) Confinement, especially during a war.

loyalty (LOI uhl tee) The strong support of one's family, country, or friends.

National Coalition for Redress and Reparations (NASH uh nuhl koh uh LISH uhn for ri DRESS and REP uh RAY shun) A group set up to demand repayment for the ills suffered by those interned by the U.S. Government during World War II.

terrorized (TER uh rized) Caused great fear to someone.

U.S. Constitution (YOO nite uhd STATESS KON stuh TOO shuhn) The written document that spells out the way the United States is governed and laws are made.

Veteran's Administration (VET ur uhnz ad MIN uh STRAY shuhn) A government group that handles the affairs of former military people.

—15—
Dolores Huerta:
Activist for Migrant Workers

by Marty Darragh

$\mathcal{D}$olores won the second prize in a national Girl Scout essay contest. Her prize was a trip. Her teachers gave her permission for time off. But the Dean of Girls said, "No." Dolores was the first Mexican-American to win the prize. In the past, white girls who had won had been given time off. Dolores was a senior in high school. This was her first taste of **racism**.

· · · · ୧୬ · · · ·

Dolores was born in Dawson, New Mexico in 1930. She was the third generation of her family to be born in New Mexico. After her parents divorced, Dolores moved to Stockton, California with her mother and two brothers. Her mother, Alicia, worked two jobs to support them. She saved her money. Finally, she was able to buy a hotel. From her mother, Dolores learned that women can be successful.

Dolores went to college to get a teaching certificate. She taught elementary school, but she soon left her job. She said, "I couldn't stand seeing farm worker's children come to class hungry and in need of shoes. I thought I could do more by organizing their parents than by trying to teach hungry children."

TIDBITS

In 1955, she co-founded the Stockton chapter of the Community Service Organization (CSO). This was a self-help group spreading across California. She wanted to help **migrant farm workers**. One of her jobs in the CSO was to ask government officials to improve local living conditions. In 1960 she founded the Agricultural Workers Association (AWA).

The CSO's founder, Fred Ross, introduced Dolores to Cesar Chavez. He was the National Director of CSO. Chavez and Huerta wanted to organize the farm workers into a union. The CSO turned them down. Dolores and her seven children moved to Delano, California. Chavez lived there. Together they founded the National Farm Workers Association (NFWA) in 1962. This would later become the United Farm Workers (UFW). They began to organize the workers into a union.

In 1965 **Filipino** grape workers left their jobs. They were on **strike** for higher pay. The NFWA voted to join the strike. Chavez asked the public to **boycott** grapes. People all over America stopped buying grapes. This was the first successful strike by farm workers. The strike continued until 1970.

During the boycott, Dolores represented the union in contract talks. The first contract was with the Schenley Wine Company in 1966. The contracts gave the workers medical benefits and retirement money. They also required growers to stop using harmful **pesticides**. Workers exposed to these chemicals often became ill.

The UFW kept organizing grape workers. It started to organize other farm workers. Huerta asked the Federal government to end farm "guest worker" programs. Through these programs, workers came to America's farms to work. They paid taxes but could not become citizens. Dolores's efforts worked. The Immigration Act of 1985 was passed. Then 1,400,000 farm workers were granted **amnesty**. They were allowed to stay in America and become citizens.

During the 1965 UFW grape strike in Delano, California Dolores stood on the top of a car, raised her sign, and urged workers in the fields to join the strike.

In 2002, Dolores won the Nation/Puffin Award for Creative Citizenship. With the $100,000 award, she started the Dolores Huerta Foundation. The foundation trains people to be organizers. Dolores is the president of the foundation. She continues to work for social justice.

TIDBITS

Dolores has been arrested more than 20 times for her activism. While she was passing out press releases in 1988, she was badly beaten by police. She had broken ribs and needed emergency surgery to remove her spleen.

The Dolores Huerta Foundation's mission is "To inspire and motivate people to organize sustainable communities to attain social justice."

Timeline: Dolores Huerta

1930	➤	Dolores Clara is born on April 10 to Juan Fernandez and Alicia Chavez Fernandez in Dawson, New Mexico.
1933	➤	Dolores's parents divorce.
1936	➤	Her mother moves Dolores and her two brothers to Stockton, California.
1947	➤	Dolores graduates from high school.
1950	➤	Dolores marries her first husband, Ralph Head. The marriage does not last.
1955	➤	Co-founds the Stockton chapter of the Community Service Organization. Marries Ventura Huerta.
1960	➤	Dolores co-founds the Agricultural Workers Association.
1962	➤	With Cesar Chavez, starts the National Farm Workers Association.
1965	➤	Directs the United Farm Workers' grape boycott.
1966	➤	The contract between the United Farm Workers Organizing Committee and Schenley Wine Company is signed.
1969	➤	Marries Richard Chavez, Cesar Chavez's brother.
1970	➤	Signs a **collective bargaining** agreement with grape growers.
1974	➤	Farm workers get unemployment benefits based on work Dolores does.
1975	➤	California passes a law giving farm workers the right to bargain for better pay.
1984	➤	Dolores gets the Outstanding Labor Leader Award from the California state senate.
1985	➤	She works to have The Immigration Act of 1985 passed.
1988	➤	Dolores is seriously beaten by police while protesting in San Francisco.
1993	➤	Dolores is elected to the National Women's Hall of Fame. She also gets the Roger Baldwin Medal of Liberty, the Eugene V. Debs Foundation Outstanding American Award, the Ellis Island Medal of Freedom, and the Consumers' Union Trumpeter's Award.
1998	➤	President Bill Clinton gives her the United States Presidential Eleanor Roosevelt Human Rights Award.
2002	➤	She receives the Nation/Puffin Award for Creative Citizenship. She uses the $100,000 award money to start the Dolores Huerta Foundation.

Learn More About Dolores Huerta and the Migrant Farm Workers

- Doak, Robin S. *Dolores Huerta: Labor Leader and Civil Rights Activist (Signature Lives).* Compass Point Books, 2008.
- Kent, Deborah. *Migrant Farm Workers: Hoping for a Better Life (A Proud Heritage: the Hispanic Library).* Child's World, 2005.
- Miller, Debra A. *Dolores Huerta, Labor Leader (The Twentieth Century's Most Influential: Hispanics).* Lucent Books, 2006.

Web sites:

- The Dolores Huerta Foundation web site:
  http://www.doloreshuerta.org/
- United Farm Workers:
  http://www.ufw.org/

Glossary

amnesty (AM nuh stee) An official promise by a government to release prisoners or pardon crimes.

boycott (BOI kot) To refuse to buy something or take part in something as a way of making a protest.

collective bargaining (kuh LEKT uhv BAR guhn ing) Discussions between an employer and a union. A collective bargaining agreement allows these discussions to take place.

Filipino (fil uh PEE no) The name given to a native of the Philippines.

migrant farm workers (MYE gruhnt farm WUR kurz) People who move from farm to farm to help harvest crops. Many of these workers are immigrants from other countries.

pesticides (PESS tuh sidez) Chemicals used to kill insect pests.

racism (RAY si zuhm) Acting as if one race of people is better than another; treating people of another race unfairly.

strike (STRIKE) To refuse to work because of a disagreement with an employer over work hours, wages, or other issues.

Dian Fossey:
Protector of the Mountain Gorilla

by Linda Crotta Brennan

Dian Fossey had worked for years to gain the trust of her mountain gorillas. Now an impish young male, Peanuts, strutted toward her. Dian scratched her head. Peanuts scratched his.

Dian lay back, stretching her arm toward him. For a few moments, Peanuts stared at her upturned hand. Then he reached out and brushed her fingers with his own.

Beating his chest in excitement, Peanuts ran off to rejoin his family. Tears streamed down Dian's face.

· · · · ◯◯ · · · ·

In many ways, Dian Fossey felt closer to mountain gorillas than to humans. Her parents divorced when she was three. After that, she rarely saw her father. Her mother remarried, and her stepfather was a strict and distant man. Often alone, Dian had a hard time making friends.

Dian loved animals, but her parents forbade pets. When she went to college, she studied to be a vet. Unfortunately, science gave her trouble. Instead she became an **occupational therapist** working with disabled children.

Taking out a loan, Dian went on her dream vacation, an African **safari.** Her guide took her to Dr. Louis Leakey's **archeological digs**. While there, she tripped and broke her ankle. But Dian wouldn't let that spoil her trip. She continued to her next stop, climbing mountains to see gorillas. Dian was fascinated by these magnificent animals.

After Dian returned home, she learned that Dr. Leakey was giving a lecture nearby. She went to hear him. Dr. Leakey remembered her and her determination to see the gorillas, in spite of her hurt ankle. He offered her a job studying mountain gorillas.

She set up her first **research station** in a mountain meadow in the Congo. But the Congo was in the middle of a civil war. Dian was only there six months when soldiers attacked. She was taken prisoner. Promising the soldiers money, she escaped over the border into Uganda.

But Dian didn't give up. She set up another research station in the mountains of Rwanda. She called it Karisoke.

In order to get close enough to the gorillas to study them, Dian acted like one. She crouched down, pretending to eat plants. She learned to make calming gorilla sounds when she cared for two sick baby gorillas.

As Dian was accepted by the gorillas, she made special friends among them. Her favorite was Digit. She watched him grow from a "bright-eyed ball of fluff," to a mature young male.

Unfortunately, Rwanda was a poor country. Herders grazed their cattle in the mountain gorillas' **habitat. Poachers** hunted

TIDBITS

Dr. Louis Leakey, an archeologist who studied early human fossils, thought that we could learn about how early humans behaved by studying apes like chimpanzees, gorillas, and orangutans.

The National Geographic Society funded Dian's research. The Society sent photographers out to take pictures of her with the gorillas. One, Bob Campbell, caught Peanuts' first touch on film.

animals to eat or sell. Dian worried that her mountain gorillas would soon be extinct. She fought to protect them. She drove herdsmen out of the forest. She collected traps and scared away poachers by pretending to be a witch.

When her beloved Digit was killed by poachers, Dian turned to stronger methods. She established the Digit Fund to raise money. She used it to hire armed men to protect the gorillas. She killed cattle, kidnapped **intruders**, and fired guns at poachers.

Dian made many enemies. On Christmas night, 1985, someone broke into her cabin and killed her. She was buried in her gorilla graveyard, next to her dear friend Digit. The mystery of her murder was never solved.

Dian Fossey might be gone, but her **conservation movement** lives on. Because of her efforts, the mountain gorillas survive.

Dian Fossey is shown with some of the gorillas she studied.

Timeline: Dian Fossey

1932 ➤ January 16, born near San Francisco, CA, only child of George and Kitty Fossey.

1938 ➤ Her parents divorce.

1939 ➤ Her mother marries a wealthy businessman, Richard Price.

1954 ➤ Graduates college. Takes job as Occupational Therapist at Kosair Children's Hospital in Kentucky.

1963 ➤ Visits Africa, meets Dr. Louis Leakey and sees mountain gorillas.

1966 ➤ March, attends Louis Leakey's lecture, talks to him about becoming his gorilla researcher.

December, sets up research camp in Kabara Meadow, Virunga National Park, Democratic Republic of Congo.

1967 ➤ July 9, taken off mountain by armed guards and kept hostage.

July 26, escapes into Uganda.

September 24, sets up new research station at Karisoke in Parc National des Volcans in the Virunga Mountains of Rwanda.

1968 ➤ Bob Campbell arrives to photograph gorillas for National Geographic.

1969 ➤ Cares for two sick, captured baby gorillas, Pucker Puss and Coco.

1970 ➤ Peanuts touches Fossey's hand.

1976 ➤ Earns PhD in zoology from Darwin College, Cambridge in England.

1977 ➤ Digit killed by poachers. Dian establishes Digit Fund to raise money for anti-poacher patrols.

1980 ➤ Teaches at Cornell University in New York.

1983 ➤ Publishes book, *Gorillas in the Mist.*

1985 ➤ December 26, murdered in cabin at Karisoke. She was 53.

Learn More about Dian Fossey

- Gogerly, Liz. ***Dian Fossey.*** Raintree Steck-Vaughn Publishers, 2003.
- Mara, Wil. ***Dian Fossey: Among the Gorillas.*** Franklin Watts, 2004.
- Nicholson, Lois P. ***Dian Fossey: Primatologist.*** Chelsea House Publishers, 2003.
- Wood, Richard and Sara. ***Dian Fossey.*** Heinemann Library, 2001.

Web site:

- Dian Fossey Gorilla Fund:
  http://www.gorillafund.org/

Glossary

archeological digs (ar kee AW law juh kuhl DIGZ) Large holes dug for the purpose of searching for ancient relics.

conservation movement (KON sur VAY shuhn MOOV muhnt) An organization for the protection of wildlife, plant life, or other natural resources.

habitat (HAB uh TAT) The place and natural conditions in which a plant or an animal lives.

intruder (in TROOD uhr) A person who forces his way into a place or situation.

occupational therapist (OK yuh PAY shuhn uhl THER uh pist) A person who helps people recover from illness or injury by having them do special activities.

research station (REE surch STAY shuhn) A place from which scientific studies are carried out.

poacher (POHCH ur) A person who hunts or fishes illegally.

safari (SUH fah REE) A trip taken, especially to Africa, to hunt or photograph wild animals.

Maxine Hong Kingston: Writer of the Chinese-American Experience

by Diane Mayr

When Maxine Hong started school, the American way of doing things confused her. Not knowing how to speak English, she decided not to speak at all. "During the first silent year I spoke to no one at school, did not ask before going to the lavatory, and flunked kindergarten."

· · · · ∽ · · · ·

Ting Ting Hong was born in Stockton, California to immigrant parents. In China, her father had been a scholar and a poet. Her mother had been a doctor. In America they worked in a laundry and did farm work. Ting Ting's father gave her the English name, Maxine.

Her mother told Maxine stories of strong Chinese women such as Fa Mu Lan. She heard tales of ghosts. "Night after night my mother would talk-story until we fell asleep. I could not tell where the stories left off and the dreams began."

Maxine learned how her family came to settle in America. These stories told of great difficulties and **discrimination**. Although they were now in America,

TIDBITS

"When the thermometer in our laundry reached one hundred and eleven degrees on summer afternoons, either my mother or my father would say that it was time to tell another ghost story so that we could get some good chills up our backs." from *The Woman Warrior.*

When she was 15 years old, her essay, "I Am an American," won a prize and was printed in the Girl Scouts' magazine, *American Girl.*

her parents continued their Chinese traditions. The tales and traditions inspired Maxine to write.

Maxine may have failed kindergarten, but she later did well in school. She won 11 scholarships that allowed her to go to the University of California (UC), Berkeley. After graduating, she returned to UC to earn a teaching certificate. She has been teaching ever since.

During the Vietnam war years, Maxine took part in the peace movement. She and her husband Earll became uneasy with the increasing violence in America. They decided to leave the country. On the way to Asia, they stopped in Hawaii. They stayed there for 17 years.

While in Hawaii, Maxine wrote her two most famous books, *The Woman Warrior* and *China Men.* These books tell of Maxine's life as a Chinese-American. They also tell about her parents' and relatives' journeys to America.

Maxine's books were a mix of truth and fiction. She wrote, "There were secrets never to be said...secrets whose telling could get us sent back to China." She was careful not to make the truth too clear to her readers. She did not want to put anyone in danger of being **deported**.

She and Earll moved back to California. Her novel, *Tripmaster Monkey*, was published in 1989. She wanted to write another novel to continue the story of the characters. She worked on it for nearly two years. Then her father died. Maxine was at her father's memorial service when a wildfire broke out in the Oakland/Berkeley area. It destroyed her home. The book she had been working on was gone.

After the fire, Maxine went to search the ashes of her home. The total destruction reminded Kingston of what happens in war. She shared a sense of loss with war **veterans** and their families. In 1993 she started a group called the Veterans' Writing Group. She helps them "to find their way home through art and through writing."

Instead of trying to rewrite the book that burned, Kingston started over again. The new book combined the original story with a record of her experiences during and after the wildfire. One section is "a call to war veterans to help write a literature of peace." Maxine published *The Fifth Book of Peace* in 2003, 12 years after the fire.

Nowadays, Kingston writes poetry. She continues her work as a teacher, and with veterans. She also works for peace in the world.

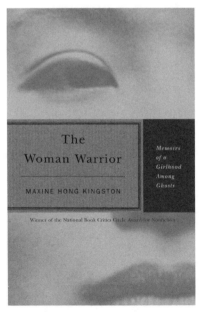

The cover of Maxine Hong Kingston's first book.

TIDBITS

At UC, Berkeley, Maxine started as an engineering student. She did not like it. She next tried **journalism**. She decided she preferred creative writing over reporting.

◆

There has been some disagreement over where her books should be shelved in a library. Are the books fiction or are they nonfiction? Maxine said, "I never defined the **genre**. I just called it a book."

Timeline: Maxine Hong Kingston

1940 ➤	October 27 is born in Stockton, California to parents Tom Hong and Ying Lan (Brave Orchid) Chew Hong. She is the oldest of six American-born children. Maxine never knew the brother and sister who had been born and died in China.
1962 ➤	Graduates from UC, Berkeley. On November 23, marries Earll Kingston, an actor.
1964 ➤	Son, Joseph Lawrence Chung Mei is born.
1963 ➤	Earns a teaching certificate from UC, Berkeley.
1967 ➤	Leaves California and ends up settling with her family in Hawaii.
1976 ➤	Publishes her first book, *The Woman Warrior: Memoirs of a Girlhood Among Ghosts*. It wins the National Book Critics Circle Award for Nonfiction.
1980 ➤	Publishes her second book, *China Men*. *China Men* wins the National Book Award for general fiction in 1981.
1984 ➤	Returns to the mainland U.S. Travels to China for the first time. She finds it like the China she had imagined based on her parents' stories.
1989 ➤	Publishes her first true novel, *Tripmaster Monkey: His Fake Book*.
1991 ➤	Her father dies in September. In October, on the day of his memorial service, a wildfire destroys her home.
1993 ➤	Forms the Veterans' Writing Group. She selects and **edits** the group's writing for an **anthology** called *Veterans of War, Veterans of Peace*, which is published in 2006.
1997 ➤	Is awarded the National **Humanities** Medal by President Bill Clinton.
2002 ➤	Publishes *To Be a Poet*.
2003 ➤	*The Fifth Book of Peace* is published.
2008 ➤	Is awarded the National Book Foundation's Medal for Distinguished Contribution to American **Letters**.

Learn More About Maxine Hong Kingston, Chinese-American Culture, and Writing

- Anderson, Dale. *Chinese Americans.* Rourke, 2008.
- Fletcher, Ralph. *How Writers Work: Finding a Process That Works for You.* HarperCollins, 2000.
- San Souci, Robert D. *Fa Mulan: The Story of a Woman Warrior.* Hyperion, 1998.

Web sites:

- Asian Pacific Fund. Yeh, Emerald. "Maxine Hong Kingston." http://www.asianpacificfund.org/awards/bio_kingston.shtml
- Smithsonian Institution. "On Gold Mountain: A Chinese American Experience." http://www.apa.si.edu/ongoldmountain

Glossary

anthology (an THOL uh jee) A collection of stories or poems, by different authors, published in one book.

deported (di PORT uhd) Sent back to the country of one's birth.

discrimination (DISS krim i NAY shuhn) Prejudice or unjust behavior to others based on differences in age, race, gender, or religion.

edits (ED itss) Checks a piece of writing for spelling or grammar errors; shortens pieces that are too long.

genre (JAN ruh) A type of category of writing, art, or music.

humanities (hyoo MAN uh teez) Subjects of study outside of math or science such as history, literature, or the arts.

journalism (JUR nuhl iz uhm) The work of gathering and reporting news for newspapers or TV.

letters (LET turz) Written works of fiction and nonfiction, not messages between people.

veterans (VET ur uhnz) People who served in the military, especially during a war.

—18—
Nancy Pelosi:
First Woman Speaker of the House

by M. Lu Major

*I*t was time for the vote. The result would not be a surprise. Usually, the political party with the most members won. This time, the Democratic Party held the most seats in the House of Representatives. Their candidate would become the new **Speaker of the House**. Still, everyone knew this vote would be like no other. Today, history would be made. Nancy Pelosi would become the first woman in the United States to lead the House.

· · · · ❧ · · · ·

Nancy D'Alessandro was born on March 26, 1940 in Baltimore, Maryland. Her mother, Anunciata, was a homemaker and volunteer. Nancy's father, Thomas, represented Maryland in **Congress** for 10 years. Later he became mayor of Baltimore. Nancy grew up with politics.

Nancy was the only girl in a family of six children. Her family believed being in politics meant helping the community. By age 13, Nancy could assist her friends and their families. She listened to their problems. Through her parents, Nancy learned how to show people where to get health care or look for jobs.

In 1958, Nancy left Baltimore to attend Trinity College in Washington, D.C. While at Trinity, she joined many clubs, including the Young Democrats. This club worked for President Kennedy's **campaign**.

After graduation, Nancy married Paul Pelosi. Paul worked in business and banking. The Pelosis had five children, 4 girls and one boy. Nancy stayed home to care for them. The family moved to San Francisco in 1969. Nancy continued to be involved in politics. She worked on campaigns. She became Chairwoman of the Northern California Democratic Party.

Nancy says that being the mother of a large family prepared her for life in politics. She learned to be very organized. She learned how to plan her day around many activities. Nancy waited until her children were grown to run for office herself. She was 47 years old.

Nancy replaced California Congresswoman Sala Burton. Mrs. Burton had become ill. She hoped Nancy would be her **successor**. When Nancy went to Washington only 23 other women held seats in the 435-member House.

In Congress, Nancy wrote bills and helped to make bills become laws. She worked on bills for equal rights, health care, and education. She said being in Congress was all about children. We need "…to build a stronger future for the generations to come."

In 2001, Nancy was the first woman chosen to be the **Minority Whip**. The Whip tries to get members of her party to agree on bills. It is one of the most powerful positions in Congress. Nancy understood how important her job was to all women. She said,

TIDBITS

More than 13,000 people have served in Congress since the United States began. Only 2% have been women.

◆

The House of Representatives has two Whips. The Majority Whip is from the political party with the most members. The Minority Whip is from the party with the fewest members.

◆

Nancy was the first Californian and the first Italian American to become Speaker of the House.

TIDBITS

The name "whip" comes from English fox hunting. It was the person who kept the hunting dogs under control.

◆—◆

The Speaker of the House is said to be "two heart beats away" from the presidency. If both the President and the Vice President died, the Speaker of the House would become President.

"We have made history. Now we must make progress."

The Minority Whip works with the Minority Leader. One year later, Nancy became the Minority Leader of the House. Again, this was the first time a woman had held this post.

After the 2006 elections, the Democrats became the **majority** party. It was time to select a new Speaker of the House. The Speaker runs Congress. It is the only leadership position named in the U.S. Constitution.

Nancy invited her children and grandchildren to see her swearing-in ceremony. She saw her new position as a reason to bring people together. The day she took office she said, "In this House, we may be different parties, but we serve one country."

Speaker of the House Nancy Pelosi meets with President Barack Obama.

Timeline: Nancy Pelosi

1940 ➤ March 26, born to Thomas and Anunciata D'Alessandro in Baltimore, Maryland.

1962 ➤ Graduated from Trinity College, Washington, D.C.

1963 ➤ September 7, marries Paul Frank Pelosi of San Francisco, California.

1964–1970 ➤ Her five children are born.

1969 ➤ Nancy and Paul Pelosi move to San Francisco, California.

1977 ➤ Elected Democratic Party Chairwoman for Northern California.

1987 ➤ Elected to represent the 8th Congressional District of California.

2001 ➤ First woman elected House Minority Whip, the second in command to the House Minority Leader.

2002 ➤ Elected to replace Dick Gephart as House Minority Whip when he decides to run for President of the United States.

2003–2007 ➤ Becomes Minority Leader of the House of Representatives.

2006 ➤ November 16, unanimously chosen as the Democratic candidate for Speaker of the House.

2007 ➤ January 3, elected Speaker of the House.
Visits Israel and Syria on a fact-finding mission.

2008 ➤ Named Permanent Chair of the 2008 Democratic National Convention in Denver, Colorado.

Learn More About Speaker Nancy Pelosi and National Government

- Dubois, Muriel L. *The U.S. House of Representatives (First Facts).* Capstone Press, 2004.

- Leavitt, Amie Jane. *Nancy Pelosi (Blue Banner Biographies).* Mitchell Lane Publishers, 2008.

Web sites:

- Speaker Nancy Pelosi's official web site:
  http://www.speaker.gov/kids

- What is the job of the Speaker of the House?
  http://www.speaker.gov/about?id = 0003

- What are Majority and Minority Whips?
  http://clerkkids.hous.gov/congress/leadership.html

Glossary

campaign (kam PAYN) A series of organized activities set up over a certain amount of time in order to win an election.

Congress (KONG griss) The governing body of the United States that makes laws. Congress is made up of the Senate and the House of Representatives.

majority (muh JOR uh tee) More than half the number of people in a group.

Minority Whip (myye NOR uh tee WIP) The person in the U.S. House of Representatives who serves as the leader of the smaller of the two political parties.

Speaker of the House (SPEE kur of the HOUSS) The officer in charge of the United States House of Representatives.

successor (suhk SESS ur) One who follows another in a position.

— 19 —
Janice Mirikitani:
Word Warrior

by Joyce Ray

Count our numbers,

harvest our strength,

breathe between the rain.

We shall not go into their camps again.

  —Janice Mirikitani, from "Breathe Between the Rain"

Janice Mirikitani stared at the black and white photo. A 3-year-old girl in a thin dress looked back at her. The girl stood by a run-down building. Her shoes scuffed the dirt. But her smoothed hair shone jet black.

Janice was the girl. She knew the U.S. government had sent Japanese Americans to **internment** camps during World War II. Her mother said the women styled each other's hair to keep their self-respect. But her mother said nothing else. The Japanese idea of *enryo* taught her to keep her thoughts to herself. Janice wanted to break the silence.

· · · · ⟳ · · · ·

Japan bombed Pearl Harbor, Hawaii in December, 1941. Many Americans were afraid. They didn't trust Japanese Americans. In March, 1942, President Franklin Roosevelt gave an order. He sent

TIDBITS

One of Janice's poems, "In Remembrance," talks about her Uncle Minoru. In the internment camp, he attracted wild birds who ... "could smell the wounds hiding in your throat, / the wound in your heart / pierced by unjust punishment, **racism** and rejection / sharp as blades."

120,000 Japanese Americans to ten barbed-wire camps. Those people lost their homes, businesses, and belongings. They had no rights, even though most were U.S. citizens.

Life was difficult in the camps. Janice was a baby at Rohwer Camp in Arkansas. Mosquitoes swarmed. The wood and tar-paper barracks were hot in summer, cold in winter. Crowded rooms had no privacy or plumbing. The women hand washed laundry and the men cut trees for fuel. Everyone worked to survive.

After Rowher closed, life was still hard. Janice was three. She was a U.S. citizen, a *Sansei* in Japanese. Sansei are Japanese Americans whose parents were also born in the U.S. The American-born parents are called *Nisei*. After the war, some people mistreated Japanese Americans. Janice's family moved to Chicago to escape **prejudice**.

Her parents divorced when Janice was five. Her mother worked three jobs. Janice spent afternoons at the movies. Her mother's remarriage and a move back to California caused more trouble. Here, Janice's stepfather and relatives abused her. For eleven years, Janice felt unsafe. She was too ashamed to tell anyone.

School was an escape from fear. Janice became a top student. In college, she tried beauty contests and cheerleading. She wanted to be accepted like white girls. Janice bleached her face. She taped her eyelids to change their shape.

Finally, Janice accepted her Asian background. She wrote poetry to change the **stereotype** of Asian women. Her poem

"Breaking Silence" challenges readers to speak out:

"We must recognize ourselves at last.

We are a rainforest of color and noise."

Janice uses words to fight injustice. She has also worked over forty years to stop it. In 1965, Janice began working at Glide Memorial United Methodist Church in San Francisco. She later became secretary. The church helped those who had been abused by police. Teens who needed help went there. People of all races gathered there.

These people helped Janice to understand herself. Since 1969, Janice has directed Glide's community programs Over 80 programs help low income people. Glide serves one million free meals a year. Its programs help school drop-outs, drug addicts and the homeless. Janice holds support groups for abused girls and women. She teaches them that together their voices are strong.

Janice listens to people's stories. Then she breaks her own silence. She writes about taboo topics – subjects that make people uncomfortable. San Francisco's mayor named Janice **Poet Laureate** of San Francisco in 2000. Janice loves poetry and has an **activist** spirit. She is a word warrior.

Janice wants her poetry to help fight injustice.

Timeline: Janice Mirikitani

1942 ➤ February 5, Janice is born to Ted and Shigemi Matsuda Mirikitani in Stockton, CA.

1942–1945 ➤ Is interned with family at Rowher Internment Camp, Arkansas.

1962 ➤ Graduates from UCLA.

1963 ➤ Receives teaching certificate from University of California at Berkeley.

1964–1965 ➤ Teaches English, speech and dance at the Contra Costa Unified School District. Begins graduate studies in creative writing at San Francisco State University.

1965 ➤ Works at Glide Church/Urban Center in San Francisco.

1966 ➤ Marries. The marriage does not last.

1967 ➤ Daughter Tianne Tsukiko Miller is born.

1968–1969 ➤ Participates in San Francisco State Third World Students' Strike.

1969 ➤ Directs community outreach programs at Glide Memorial Methodist Church.

1972 ➤ Lectures in Japanese American literature and creative writing at SF State.

1975–1989 ➤ Edits *Aion Magazine* and anthologies, including *AYUMI: A Japanese American Anthology (1980)*, *Making Waves: An Anthology by and about Asian American Women (1989)* and co-edits *I Have Something to say about This Big Trouble: Children of the Tenderloin Speak* Out (1989).

1987–1995 ➤ Publishes *Awake in the River*, *Shedding Silence* (1987), *We the Dangerous* (1995).

1982 ➤ Marries the Rev. Cecil Williams, minister of Glide Memorial Church, San Francisco.

1983 ➤ Becomes president of the Glide Foundation.

1983–present ➤ Receives many awards: Woman Warrior in Arts and Culture Award (1983), Woman of Words Award (1985), University of California at San Francisco Chancellor's Medal of Honor with Cecil Williams, "Woman of the Year" by CA State Assembly (1988), Outstanding Leadership award of the Japanese Community Youth Council (1990).

2000 ➤ Is appointed San Francisco's Poet Laureate.

2002 ➤ Publishes *Love Works*.

Learn More About Janice Mirikitani, Japanese American Internmen, and Writing Poetry

- Bunting, Eve. *So Far From the Sea.* Clarion, 1998.
- Cooper, Michael L. *Remembering Manzanar.* Clarion, 2002.
- Kadohata, Cynthia. *Weedflower.* Atheneum Books for Young Readers, 2006.
- Uchida, Yoshiko. *Journey to Topaz.* Heyday Books, 2004.

Web sites:

- Information about Janice's work at Glide Memorial Church:
  http://glide.org/
- Information about Rohwer Internment Camp from Arkansas Educational Television Network's WW II Oral History Project:
  http://www.intheirwords.org/the_home_front_experience/internment_camps/rohwer_internment_camp
- Poetry writing tips from children's poet Kristine O'Connell George:
  http://www.kristinegeorge.com/kids_tips_01.html

Glossary

activist (AK tiv ist) A person who participates in actions to change government or social conditions.

enryo (EN ry oh) In the Japanese culture, not saying or doing what you would like in order not to embarrass yourself or others.

internment (in TURN muhnt) Forced confinement particularly during a time of war.

poet laureate (POH uht   LAW ree uht) A position of honor given to a poet by a state or country.

prejudice (PREJ uh diss) An unfair opinion about someone because of the person's race, religion, or other characteristic.

priority (prye OR uh tee) Something that is more important or more urgent than other things.

racism (ray siz uhm) Treating people of other races as if they were inferior.

stereotype (stirh EE oh TIPE) An overly simple opinion of a person, group, or thing.

—20—
Billie Jean King:
Tennis Ace and Activist

by Marty Darragh

When Billie Jean was 5, she said, "I'm going to do something great with my life."

"That's nice," her mother said.

Billie Jean took her first tennis lesson when she was 11. Later, her mother picked her up. Billie Jean said, "I'm going to be number 1 in the world."

"That's nice," her mother said.

Billie Jean went on to do both.

· · · · Ꮗ · · · ·

Billie Jean Moffitt was born on November 22, 1943 in Long Beach, California. Her father was a firefighter and her mother was a homemaker.

After her first tennis lesson, Billie Jean played every chance she got. Nine months later she entered the Southern California Junior Championships. She lost the second match. Tennis was going to be a lot of work!

Billie Jean did work hard. By age 15, she was number 19 in the U.S. She took special lessons and improved to become number 4.

In 1961, Billie Jean and Karen Hantze were the youngest team to win a Women's Doubles Championship at **Wimbledon**. They were both 18.

Billie Jean kept improving. In 1964, she became a full-time athlete. She was ranked number 2. That wasn't good enough for her. Billie Jean studied in Australia with a tennis star. He taught her tennis **strategy**.

1965 was an important year. Billie Jean lost the Wimbledon Singles again. She also lost the U.S. Open. Those losses taught her what she was missing. She needed more trust in herself that she *would* win.

The next year Billie Jean finally won the Wimbledon Women's Singles Championship. But, she still wasn't number 1. It happened the next year. She won the Women's Singles, Women's Doubles and Mixed Doubles Championships at both Wimbledon and the U.S. Open.

Next, Billie Jean worked to change attitudes about tennis players. **Professional** players earned prize money when they won. Most players were **amateurs**. The big **tournaments** only allowed amateurs to enter. She spoke out about this practice. Others agreed tournaments should be open to all players and offer prize money.

In 1968 American and British tennis **associations** agreed to allow professionals to enter tournaments. Billie Jean and others turned professional. Starting that year prize money was given. This change attracted the best players. Unfortunately, prize money became a big issue. Men received more money than women. Billie Jean was furious. Gladys Heldman, Billie Jean's friend, offered

TIDBITS

Billie Jean earned money doing odd jobs to buy a **racquet** for her first tennis lesson. It cost $8.00 and had maroon strings.

• ◆ •

In 1955, she was not allowed to be photographed with other junior players after a tournament because she was wearing shorts instead of a skirt. Her mother made her tennis clothes.

TIDBITS

Billie Jean is the only woman to win U.S. Open Single Championships on all four surfaces (grass, clay, carpet, and hard).

• ◆ •

Five times, between 1966 and 1972, she was ranked number one. She was in the top ten seventeen times beginning in 1960.

to help. Heldman edited *World Tennis Magazine*. She organized a tournament for women. One tournament grew into a series. Billie Jean won 13 of the 14 tournaments in 1971. She was the first woman athlete to earn over $100,000 in one year.

In 1972 Billie Jean helped get Title IX passed. This bill forced schools to offer equal opportunities in education and sports to boys *and* girls. President Nixon signed the bill that summer.

Bobby Riggs, a 1939 Wimbledon champion, challenged Billie Jean to a match. The match took place on September 20, 1973. It was called the "Battle of the Sexes." All of Billie Jean's accomplishments were at risk. Many people still believed women athletes should not receive equal treatment. About 50,000,000 people watched the match on television. Billie Jean won.

She won her twentieth Wimbledon championship in 1979. She broke the record for most Wimbledon wins.

Billie Jean King has spent her life fighting for equality for men and women in sports and in society at large.

In 1979, Billie Jean broke the record for the most wins at the Wimbledon. The record held until 2003.

Time Line: Billie Jean King

1943	➤	November 22, Billie Jean is born in Long Beach, California. Her parents are Bill and Betty (Jerman) Moffitt.
1954	➤	She takes her first tennis lesson.
1958	➤	She is the Southern California Junior Champion.
1961	➤	She wins the Wimbledon Women's Doubles Championship with Karen Hantze. At 18, they are the youngest ever to win.
1964	➤	Mervyn Rose teaches Billie Jean in Australia. She decides to play tennis full time.
1965	➤	Billie Jean graduates from college and marries Larry King.
1966	➤	She wins the Wimbledon Women's Singles Championship.
1967	➤	Billie Jean is the Wimbledon Women's Singles, Wimbledon Women's Doubles and Wimbledon Mixed Doubles Champion. Associated Press names her "Woman Athlete of the Year."
1971	➤	She becomes the first woman athlete to earn more than $100,000 in one year.
1972	➤	Billie Jean helps Title IX to pass. It is signed by President Nixon.
1973	➤	She founds the Women's Tennis Association and is its President. Billie Jean beats Bobby Riggs in the "Battle of the Sexes." Through her efforts, the U.S. Open gives equal prize money to men and women.
1975	➤	Billie Jean wins her last Wimbledon Women's Singles Championship.
1976	➤	*Time* magazine names her "Woman of the Year."
1984	➤	Billie Jean is named Commissioner of World Team Tennis, the first woman to be commissioner of a professional sport.
1987	➤	She and Larry are divorced. She is inducted into the International Tennis Hall of Fame.
2000	➤	The U.S. Olympic team wins four gold medals with her as coach.
2006	➤	The National Tennis Center is renamed the Billie Jean King National Tennis Center. An announcement is made that the Billie Jean King International Sports Center will be in the Sports Museum of American.

Learn More About Billie Jean King and Tennis

- Blumenthal, Karen. *Let Me Play: The Story of Title IX: The Law That Changed The Future of Girls in America.* Simon & Schuster Children's Publishing, 2005.

- Haun, James, Lynn Haun and Howard Schroeder. *King: The Sports Career of Billie Jean King (Sports Legends).* Crestwood House, 1981.

- Rappoport, Ken. *Ladies First: Women Athletes Who Made a Difference.* Peachtree, 2005.

- Rusch, Elizabeth. *Girls' Tennis: Conquering the Court.* Coughlan Publishing, 2007.

Web sites:

- Billie Jean King: Visionary, Innovator, Champion: http://www.billiejeanking.com/

- Hickok Sports Biographies: King, Billie Jean (Moffitt): http://www.hickoksports.com/biograph/kingbilliejean.shtml#other

Glossary

amateur (AM uh chur or AM uh tur) Someone who takes part in a sport or other activity for pleasure rather than for money.

association (uh SOH see AY shuhn) An organization, club, or a society.

professional (pruh FESH uh nuhl) Making money for doing something others do for fun, as in a professional athlete.

racquet (RAK it) A stringed frame with a handle that is used in games such as tennis, squash, or badminton.

strategy (STRAT uh jee) A clever plan for achieving a goal.

tournament (TUR nuh muhnt) A series of contests in which a number of people or teams try to win the championship.

Wimbledon (WIM bull duhn) A town outside of London, England. For over 100 years Wimbledon has been the site of an important tennis championship.

—21—
Marcy Carsey:
Television Producer

by Sally Wilkins

Marcy woke up shaking. That same nightmare again! Giant doors slamming in her face, shutting her out of television. Marcy had left a good job at ABC to start a television **production company**. A year later, she had not sold one new program. Now both the Writers' **Guild** and the Actors' Guild were on strike. Her husband John was a television writer. Marcy and John had two small children. Money was very tight. Had she made a terrible mistake?

· · · · ⌒◯ · · · ·

Marcia Lee Peterson was born in Weymouth, Massachusetts. Marcy's father worked at the Navy shipyard. Her mother stayed at home with Marcy and her brother.

In the 1950s Americans fell in love with television. Marcy's favorite shows were family comedies. She loved *Father Knows Best* and *I Remember Mama*.

After college Marcy moved to New York City. She gave tours at NBC. Soon she became a **production assistant** for *The Tonight Show*. She ran errands and helped wherever she was needed. She also met John Jay Carsey.

TIDBITS

When Marcy brought her babies to work at ABC, she dressed casually. Sometimes to dress up for board meetings she'd borrow an outfit from one of her television programs.

＊◆＊

Marcy objected to **stereotypes**. She changed Bill Cosby's character from a chauffeur to a doctor, and objected to the "dumb blonde" character in *Third Rock from the Sun.*

Although John was much older than Marcy, they married in 1969. They moved to Los Angeles. John worked as a writer and producer. Marcy read scripts for an independent production company.

Two years later Marcy heard that ABC was hiring. Marcy had just learned she was pregnant. In the early 1970s it was unusual for women to return to work while their children were small. "I can come back after I have the baby," she told Michael Eisner at her interview.

"Of course," he said. "My wife and I are having a baby, and I'm coming back." Marcy knew she was at the right company. She kept a playpen in her office. She cut meetings short to go home for dinner.

Marcy became Senior Vice President of Prime Time Series. Then ABC's management changed. Her new boss admitted he was "uncomfortable" giving women powerful positions. It was time to leave.

That first year was hard. Marcy missed working with her friends at ABC. She wondered if she would be as good at selling programs as she had been at deciding what to buy. When John asked, "Are we poor, or just out of cash?" Marcy knew it was a joke. Still, she had nightmares.

Marcy would not give up. She invited her friend Tom Werner to join her company. They rented a tiny office over a store. Experts said **sitcoms** were old-fashioned. Marcy and Tom believed people would still watch family comedies. Their motto was *"Quality over quantity - every program must be worthy of its airtime."*

Marcy persuaded Bill Cosby to make a sitcom with Carsey-Werner. ABC and CBS turned it down. NBC bought the idea but didn't give them enough money to finish production. Marcy and Tom **mortgaged** their houses to pay the bills.

The Cosby Show was a huge hit. Still in **syndication**, it is one of the most profitable television shows of all time. Soon all three **networks** were **broadcasting** Carsey-Werner shows.

Marcy Carsey is one of the most successful women in Hollywood. The Carseys welcomed guests and friends to their beautiful home. Marcy raised her children. She cared for John until he died. She brought her elderly mother to live with her.

The television business keeps changing. In 2005 Marcy started a new career in folk art. She also **mentors** young women starting businesses. Instead of dreaming of slamming doors, she opens them for other people.

Marcy loves hiking and long-distance bicycling. She and her brother have enjoyed vacations exploring France by bicycle.

•—•

Carsey-Werner's television programs have been nominated for more than 100 Emmy, Golden Globe and People's Choice awards. Marcy herself has won many awards and been named to the Academy of Television Arts and Sciences Hall of Fame.

The television shows produced by Carsey-Werner received many awards, including numerous Emmy Awards.

Timeline: Marcy Carsey

1944	➤	November 21, Marcia Lee Peterson born in Weymouth, Massachusetts to John Edwin Peterson and Rebecca White Peterson.
1966	➤	Graduates from University of New Hampshire with Bachelor of Arts degree in English Literature. Moves to New York City with friends, finds work as a tour guide at NBC.
1969	➤	April 12, marries John Jay Carsey, a television comedy writer. Moves to Los Angeles.
1974	➤	Michael Eisner at ABC television hires Marcy.
1975	➤	First child, Rebecca, born. Marcy sets up a playpen in her office at ABC.
1978	➤	Second child, Peter is born.
1980	➤	Marcy leaves ABC to start her own television production company.
1984	➤	*The Cosby Show* becomes the number one show for NBC.
1985	➤	*The Cosby Show* wins the Emmy for Best Comedy Series.
1988	➤	Carsey-Warner produces the top show on each of the three major networks (*Cosby*, *Roseanne*, and *A Different World*).
1989	➤	NAACP gives the Image Award to an episode of *A Different World*.
1990	➤	Marcy receives the Women in Film Crystal Award, "The Lucy Award."
1998	➤	Marcy joins Oprah Winfrey and Nickelodeon's Geraldine Laybourne in creation of a new cable network Oxygen Media.
2001	➤	Marcy receives the David Susskind Lifetime Achievement Award from the Producers Guild of America.
2002	➤	John Jay Carsey dies. Marcy establishes The Carsey Institute at UNH to conduct policy research on children, youth and families, and community development.
2005	➤	Marcy Carsey and Tom Werner leave CW. Tom becomes part-owner of the Boston Red Sox. Marcy opens Just Folk, a folk art gallery and store, in Malibu.

Learn More About Marcy Carsey and Working in Television

- Apel, Melanie Ann. *Cool Careers without College for Film and Television Buffs.* Rosen Publishing Group, Inc. 2002.

- Dunkleberger, Amy. *So You Want to Be a Film or TV Editor?* Enslow Publishers, 2007.

- Parish, James Robert and Allen Taylor. *Career Opportunities in Television and Cable.* Ferguson Publishing Co., 2006.

Web sites:

- The Paley Center for Media: SheMadeIt.org. Watch a video about Marcy Carsey: http://www.shemadeit.org/meet/summary.aspx?m = 19

Glossary

broadcasting (BRAWD kast ing) Sending out a program on TV or the radio.

guild (GILD) A professional group for people who do the same kind of work.

mentor (MEN tohr) A coach or guide.

mortgage (MOR gij) A loan from a bank to buy a house or business.

network (NET wurk) A system of things that are connected to each other. A television network is a group of TV stations that work together.

production assistant (pruh DUHK shuhn uh SISS tuhnt) A person who helps the producer put on a play, TV show, or movie.

production company (pruh DUHK shuhn KUHM puh nee) A group of people who work together to put on a play, TV show, or movie.

sitcom (SIT kom) Short for "situation comedy." A humorous television program that features the same group of characters each week.

stereotype (STER ee oh TIPE) An overly simple picture or opinion of a person, group, or thing.

syndication (sin duh KAY shuhn) Television programs in syndication have been sold to a group who show repeats on various TV stations.

—22—
Judith Baca:
Healing with Art

by Joyce Ray

*J*udy Baca's **mural** team was painting an L.A. park **band shell**. Rival gang members made up the team. Someone didn't want Fernando on Judy's team. He was stabbed fourteen times. After he had healed, Judy asked Fernando how he was doing. He said the scars on his chest looked like a map of violence. So Judy designed tattoos to transform his scars. An act of violence became a work of art.

· · · · ᦉ · · · ·

Judy Baca has helped heal other scars with her art. She works to heal the scars of misunderstanding between people. In the 1970s and '80s, Judy organized **ethnic** groups into teams. She encouraged them to paint their history in bold colors. City walls were their **canvasses**.

Judy's love of art began in kindergarten. She only spoke Spanish. English lessons were hard to understand at first. Her teachers gave her paints instead of class work. Judy spread paint around her paper. It smelled good. She felt like she was in the picture.

112

Judy lived with her mother, grandmother, and two aunts until she was six. Judy's mother had art talent, too. She often painted Judy's portrait. Pictures of saints and potted herbs filled Judy's home. Her Latina grandmother combined prayer and herbs for healing. Judy learned about her own Hispanic background from her grandmother. Later, Judy's art entertained others. In high school, she drew amusing chalk board pictures. At work, she made cartoons of co-workers.

In college, Judy studied history, education and art. After graduating, she taught art in East Los Angeles activity centers. She watched gangs spray-paint **graffiti** on buildings. Judy recognized talent in their **slogans** and pictures. She organized teams to decorate the parks. At first, parents and business owners opposed her plans. Few people gave money for supplies. They didn't want her to encourage graffiti.

But Judy didn't give up. She asked the teens to paint a mural with her. She listened to their ideas. Then she projected the outline onto a band shell. It was Judy's own grandmother with outstretched arms. When *"Mi Abuelita"* was finished, the parks manager made Judy Director of the Eastside Murals.

Other gangs wanted the "mural lady" in their territories. Members did not cross neighborhood boundaries without fighting. Judy wanted to change this pattern. She believed teens could respect each other by working together.

In 1976, Judy began the *Great Wall* project. The canvas was a concrete channel. The Los Angeles River once flowed there. Judy hired youth from different racial backgrounds. They

TIDBITS

SPARC, the Social and Public Art Resource Center promotes interest in murals. Artists in a lab use computers to design murals. The digital images can be transferred anywhere. Judy's recent *La Memoria De Nuestra Tierra (Our Land has Memory)*, was transferred to aluminum in Denver International Airport.

painted the history of California. For seven summers over 400 teens swished reds, oranges, blues and purples across the wall. It was one-half mile long and thirteen feet high, the longest mural in the world. Judy called it "a tattoo on the scar where the river once ran." She hoped the mural would create understanding among the young artists.

A teen suggested continuing the idea. So Judy started the *World Wall*. The *World Wall* can be moved for display. It forms a semi-circle with a 100-foot diameter. The sections are thirty feet wide and ten feet high. Artists from different countries painted their visions for a peaceful world. Artists from the U.S., Finland, Russia, and Mexico have created sections. Canada, Australia, and Brazil will be represented, too.

Judy Baca's grandmother healed with herbs and prayer. Judy prays that her art heals. "Have the biggest vision you can," she says. "If you can't dream it, it cannot occur."

Judy stands in front of the Great Wall project in Los Angeles.

Timeline: Judith Baca

1946 ► September 20, Judith Francisca Baca is born in Los Angeles to Ortensia Baca. Judy's father does not know she is born.

1952 ► Moves to Pacoima, CA with mother and new stepfather, Clarence Ferrari.

1964 ► Graduates from Bishop Alemany High School, Mission Hills, CA.

1965 ► Judy marries. The marriage ends in 1971.

1969 ► Graduates from California State University, Northridge. Begins teaching at Bishop Alemany High School.

c1970 ► Is fired, along with other teachers, for protesting the Vietnam War.

1970 ► Teaches art in the Los Angeles Department of Recreation and Parks. Directs the painting of "Mi Abuelita" in Hollenbeck Park.

1974 ► Starts Citywide Murals Program. Supervises about 250 murals painted by teens. In all, 1,000 kids paint more than 500 murals.

1976 ► Co-founds SPARC: Social and Public Art Resource Center with Christina Schlesinger and Donna Deitch.

1976–1984 ► Coordinates the *Great Wall of Los Angeles*.

1977 ► Judy studies the techniques of the Mexican muralists.

1980 ► Becomes a professor of Fine Arts at UCLA.

1988–1995 ► Judy supervises "Great Wall Unlimited: Neighborhood Pride," over ninety murals painted by youth and adult artists.

1990 ► Begins the *World Wall: A Vision of the Future Without Fear*.

1996–present ► Becomes Vice-chairperson of Cesar Chavez Center, UCLA. Professor of Art for World Arts and Cultures, UCL.

2000 ► Judy and her team work with Durango, Colorado citizens to create the digital mural, *La Memoria de Nuestra Tierra: Durango*. (The Memorial of Our Land: Durango).

2004–present ► Judy designs the Martin Luther King, Robert Kennedy, and Cesar Chavez memorials.

NOTE: c1970 means about or around 1970

Learn More About Judy Baca and Murals

- Ancona, George. *Murals: Walls That Sing*. Marshall Cavendish, 2003.
- Olmstead, Mary. *Judy Baca (Hispanic-American Biographies.)* Raintree, 2004.

Web sites:

- Judy Baca's web site:
  http://www.judybaca.com

- Painting the *Great Wall*:
  http://www.youtube.com/watch?v = tJRL_AhQ3u4

- Images of the *Great Wall, World Wall and Neighborhood Pride* murals:
  http://www.sparcmurals.org/sparcone/index.php?option = com_content&task = view&id = 42&Itemid = 74

- Murals by children in the Washington, D.C. area:
  http://www.usbg.gov/whats-happening/past-exhibits/Featured-Murals-Kids-Paint.cfm

Glossary

band shell (BAND SHEL) An outdoor stage for band performances with a covered, curved roof.

canvasses (KAN vuhss uhz) A surfaces for painting made from coarse strong cloth stretched over a wooden frame.

ethnic (ETH nik) Having to do with a group of people sharing the same national origins, language, or culture.

graffiti (gruh FEE tee) Pictures drawn or words written on the walls of buildings, on subway cars, or on other surfaces.

herb (URB) A plant used in cooking or medicine.

mi abuelita (MEE ah-boo-ay-LE-tah) Spanish phrase meaning "my grandmother."

slogan (SLOH guhn) A phrase or motto used by a business, a group, or an individual to express a goal or belief.

—23—
Sally Ride:
Astronaut and Educator

by Kathleen W. Deady

June 18, 1983 . . . 7:32 a.m.

$\mathcal{S}$ally lay strapped in her seat. She watched the lights flash across the control panel.

"T minus 35 seconds . . . seventeen seconds . . . We have main engine **ignition** . . . and lift off."

The roar of the engines filled Sally's head. A huge weight pushed her against the seat as the shuttle rose against the earth's gravity. Sally focused on her job. She didn't think about the dangers. She didn't think about the reporters and thousands of cheering spectators. Or that she was making history.

. . . . ௯௦ . . . .

Sally Ride was born May 26, 1951 in Los Angeles, and grew up in Encino, California. She was active in many sports, including swimming and baseball. When she was ten, Sally tried tennis. By twelve, she was competing in the national junior tennis circuit.

Sally went to Westlake School for Girls on a tennis **scholarship**. She was a good student, and especially liked sciences and math. At that time, it was unusual for girls to be pursuing careers in the sciences. Her parents and teachers helped her see she could do anything she wanted.

After graduation, Sally enrolled in Swarthmore College in Pennsylvania to study **physics**. In her second year, she began to question her choice. Could she have been a professional tennis player? Sally left college and trained seriously for a few months. She soon decided she was not good enough to make it.

In 1970, Sally transferred to Stanford University. By late 1977, Sally was almost finished her **Ph.D**. She wanted to be a research scientist and professor. Then something happened that changed the course of her life.

Sally saw an ad in the Stanford newspaper. **NASA** (the National Aeronautics and Space Administration) was looking for astronauts. They had always used men who were military test pilots. Now they wanted scientists to do research experiments. And women could apply. Sally knew instantly that she had to try.

Over 8,000 people applied for 35 openings. Sally was one of six women selected. She trained for a year in a wide **curriculum**. Next, she served on the ground as the **communications officer** for the second and third shuttle flights. Sally was then picked for the crew of the seventh shuttle mission.

On June 18, 1983, Sally became the first American woman in space. She and the crew used a robot arm for the first time.

They **retrieved** one satellite and launched others. They did experiments. After six days, they landed successfully on earth.

Sally returned to space again in October of 1984. In 1986, she was training for her third flight when disaster struck. The flight carrying Christa McAuliffe, the first teacher in space, exploded. All seven on the crew were killed. Sally stopped her training. She joined a panel to help investigate the accident.

Sally left NASA in 1987. She was anxious to get back to teaching. For two years, she worked at Stanford. She then became Professor of Physics at the University of California.

Over time, Sally realized that many girls lose interest in science after elementary school. She wanted to change that. In 2001, Sally formed her own company, Sally Ride Science. She creates science programs for schools to entertain and motivate students.

Sally paved the way for woman in science and space exploration. But her greatest work might be with children. She continues to inspire young people, especially girls, to be future scientists.

Sally Ride was the first American Woman in Space.

TIDBITS

Sally was the only person to investigate both the Challenger disaster in 1986 and the Columbia disaster in 2003.

•—•

Sally has worked to improve science programs in schools. She has written several science books for children, including *Exploring Our Solar System, The Mystery of Mars, The Third Planet, Voyager, and To Space and Back.*

•—•

Sally has received many awards and honors. She was awarded the NASA Space Flight Medal twice.

Timeline: Sally Ride

1951 ▸	May 26, born in Los Angeles, first child of Dr. and Mrs. Dale Ride.
1968 ▸	Graduates from Westlake School for Girls in Los Angeles.
	Enters Swarthmore College in Pennsylvania to study physics.
1969 ▸	Leaves Swarthmore in second year to pursue possible tennis career.
1970 ▸	Fall, transfers to Stanford University in Palo Alto, California.
1973 ▸	Graduates from Stanford University with two degrees, a Bachelor of Science in Physics and a Bachelor of Arts in English.
1975 ▸	Receives master's degree in Physics.
1977 ▸	Applies for astronaut position in NASA's new space shuttle program.
1978 ▸	January 16, one of six women of 35 astronaut candidates selected by NASA.
	Receives Doctorate degree (Ph.D) in Physics.
	July, begins astronaut training at Johnson Space Center in Houston.
1982 ▸	April, named one of four crew members for seventh shuttle mission.
	July, marries fellow astronaut Steven Hawley.
1983 ▸	June 18, becomes first American woman to travel into space as part of Challenger crew.
1984 ▸	Returns to space for second flight, as Mission Specialist on flight STS 41-G.
1986 ▸	January 28, Challenger explodes, killing crew, including teacher Christa McAuliffe.
	Sally stops training to help investigate accident.
1987 ▸	Founds NASA Office of Exploration before leaving NASA.
	Accepts position at Stanford Center for International Security and Arms Control.
	Divorces Steven Hawley.
1989 ▸	Becomes Physics Professor and Director of University of California Space Institute.
2001 ▸	Starts own company, Sally Ride Science.
2003–2007 ▸	Inducted into Astronaut Hall of Fame (2003), California Hall of Fame (2006) National Aviation Hall of Fame (2007).

Learn More about Sally Ride, NASA, and Space

- Kramer, Barbara. *Sally Ride, A Space Biography.* Enslow Publishers Inc., 1999.
- Orr, Tamara. *Sally Ride, The First American Woman in Space.* Rosen Publishing Group, 2004.

Web sites:

- Biography, interview, and photos:
  http://www.achievement.org/autodoc/page/rid0bio-1
- Sally Ride Science web site:
  http://www.sallyridescience.com/
- Sally's NASA Biography:
  http://www.jsc.nasa.gov/Bios/htmlbios/ride-sk.html

Glossary

communications officer (kuh MYOO nuh KAY shunz OF uh sur) A person who gives out information about current space flights.

curriculum (kuh RIK yuh luhm) A program of study for a school.

ignition (ig NISH uhn) The firing or blasting off of a rocket.

NASA The organization that trains astronauts and studies space.

Ph.D Abbreviation for Doctor of Philosophy. This is the highest college degree a person can reach.

physics (FIZ iks) The scientific study of matter and energy including force, heat, light, motion, and sound.

retrieved (ri TREEVD) Brought something back.

scholarship (SKOL ur ship) A grant of money or a prize that pays for college.

—24—
Anita L. DeFrantz:
Olympian

by Deborah Bruss

In January 1980, Anita DeFrantz was at a birthday party. She saw President Carter on TV. He was announcing that the U.S. would not participate in the Olympics.

Anita was shocked. Her eight-person rowing team had trained for four years. They were ready to compete.

The Olympics were being held in Moscow – the capital of the **USSR**. President Carter wanted the USSR to withdraw their troops from Afghanistan. He hoped that an Olympic **boycott** would work.

Anita was a lawyer. She quoted a law that said she had the right to compete. She made a speech to the United States Olympic Committee (**USOC**). "We define our liberty by testing it. This is such a test." Some members of the USOC applauded her. Still, the USOC voted with President Carter. The athletes could not go.

Anita filed a **lawsuit** against the USOC. "Only the athletes could decide," she said. She lost the lawsuit but got the attention of the International Olympic Committee (**IOC**). In 1981 the IOC gave her a special award for her leadership.

· · · · ⟡ · · · ·

Anita was born in 1952 in Pennsylvania and grew up in Indianapolis, Indiana. She watched her three brothers play high school sports. She did not play because there were no teams for girls.

Anita went to college and discovered rowing. She went to law school in 1975 and joined the Olympic rowing team in 1976. Her days were packed. She trained early in the morning, in the evening, and sometimes during lunch. She attended classes all day. Sometimes she worked all night at a police headquarters. She had to pay her own way to be part of the national team.

At the 1976 Montreal Olympics, Anita's team won the bronze medal. For the next four years she worked as a lawyer and for Princeton University. She also rowed her way to six national championships.

Anita's gold medal dreams died when the U. S. boycotted the 1980 Moscow Games. After the lawsuit, she got hate mail and **threatening** phone calls. People said that she was un-American. She was broke and nervous about her future but she never regretted her actions.

In 1981 Anita was hired by the USOC. She was in charge of the Olympic Villages for the 1984 Games. "It was like planning

TIDBITS

At Connecticut College, Anita asked a man about the long boat he was carrying. He was the coach. Since Anita was almost six feet tall, he suggested she try out for the team.

•▪•

In rowing, each rower has one oar. The boat is about 60 feet long and 22 inches wide. The "coxswain," who coaches and steers, sits in the front. An eight-person team can reach speeds of 32 feet per second.

TIDBITS

In 1857 the sliding seat was invented. Previously, rowers greased their seats and wore leather pants.

⋯

Anita says that **doping** is like stealing from other athletes. "If you don't have enough courage to face your own ability, you're a coward." With drugs, maybe she could have won gold, she said. "And maybe I could have been dead. But I know that I won this bronze medal on my own ability, and I'm proud of that...."

a town," she said. She did not like the first set of plans. Women and men on the same team were housed in separate villages. Anita insisted that they be together. "Before the change, teams had to meet outside their sections."

Millions of dollars were left over after the 1984 Los Angeles Games. Some of it was used to start the LA84 Foundation. Anita became its president in 1987. The foundation supports over 1,000 youth sports organizations and after-school programs in southern California.

Anita stayed active in the IOC and USOC. She helped bring about many changes. U.S. athletes can now accept money for training and competitions. Women compete in soccer and softball. The IOC supports athletes from poorer countries. There is better coordination between the Olympic and **Paralympic** Games.

Anita's team wins the bronze medal. She is seated third from left.

In 1997 Anita was elected Vice-President of the IOC. She was the first American woman and the first African-American in that position. Many people agree that Anita DeFrantz is the most powerful woman in the world of sports.

Timeline: Anita L. DeFrantz

1952 ➤ October 4, Anita L. DeFrantz is born in Philadelphia, Pennsylvania to Anita and Robert DeFrantz. She grows up in Indianapolis, Indiana, with three brothers.

1970 ➤ Anita graduates from a high school where there are no girls sports.

1970–1974 ➤ At Connecticut College, Anita plays basketball and joins the rowing team.

1974–1977 ➤ She attends the University of Pennsylvania Law School.

1975 ➤ Anita joins the Olympic rowing team. Her team rows an eight-person shell.

1975–1980 ➤ Her team wins 6 national championships.

1976 ➤ At the Summer Olympics in Montreal, Anita is team captain. Her team wins the bronze medal. This is the first time women are allowed to row in the Olympics.

1977 ➤ Anita works as a lawyer at the Juvenile Law Center in Philadelphia, PA.

1978 ➤ Her team wins a silver medal at the World Rowing Championships.

1979 ➤ Anita works for Princeton University. The Soviet Union invades Afghanistan.

1980 ➤ The U.S. and 61 other nations boycott the Summer Olympic Games in Moscow. Anita files a lawsuit with 14 other athletes, but loses.

1981 ➤ The IOC gives her an award for her leadership against the boycott.

1981–1985 ➤ Anita organizes and manages the Olympic Village at the University of Southern California for the 1984 Games.

1985–1990 ➤ Anita serves on the Women's Sports Foundation's Board of Trustees.

1986 ➤ She is elected to the International Olympic Committee (IOC).

1992 ➤ Anita is elected to the Executive Board of the IOC.

1995 ➤ Anita becomes chairwoman of the IOC's Women and Sport Working Group.

1997 ➤ Anita becomes the first American woman and the first African-American Vice-President since the IOC was founded in 1894.

2008 ➤ As well as Vice-President of the IOC, Anita is the President of the LA 84 Foundation, and the President of the Amateur Athletic Foundation of Los Angeles.

Learn More About Anita L. DeFrantz, Rowing, and the Olympics

- Page, Jason. *Rowing, Sailing, and Other Sports on the Water (The Olympic Sports).* Crabtree Publishing Company, 2008.
- Plowden, Martha Ward. *Olympic Black Women.* Pelican Publishing Company, 1995.

Web sites:

- Anita De Frantz, one of Sports Illustrated's 100 Greatest Female Athletes: http://sportsillustrated.cnn.com/siforwomen/top_100/56/
- Ms. Magazine interview with Anita DeFrantz: http://www.msmagazine.com/summer2004/anitadefrantz.asp
- Learn about crew and rowing: http://pbskids.org/itsmylife/body/teamsports/article4.html
- Oral histories of Olympians from Southern California: http://www.la84foundation.org/5va/oralhistory_frmst.htm

Glossary

boycott (BOI kot) To refuse to take part in something as a way of making a protest.

doping (DOHP ing) Using an illegal or addictive drug in order to perform better in athletics.

IOC – International Olympic Committee (IN tur NASH uh nuhl oh LIM pik kuh MIT ee) The governing body of the Modern Olympic Games. It was organized in 1894 for the 1896 Games.

lawsuit (LAW soot) A legal action brought against a person or group in a court of law.

Paralympic Games (PA ruh LIM pik GAMEZ) The Olympics for athletes with disabilities. Competitions take place at the same site as the Olympic Games.

threatening (THRET uhn ing) Warning that some harm will be done if a certain thing is done or not done.

USOC – United States Olympic Committee (yoo NITE uhd STAYTSS oh LIM pik kuh MIT ee) The group that monitors Olympic Athletes and sports in the U.S.

USSR – Union of Soviet Socialist Republics (YOO nee uhn of SOH vee eht SOH shul ist ree PUHB liks) Also the Soviet Union. The former name given to Russia and 15 other countries united under the rule of the Communist Party.

—25—
Maria Shriver:
Journalist and First Lady
of California

by Andrea Murphy

*I*t was 1972. Maria's father was running for Vice President of the United States. Sixteen-year-old Maria **campaigned** with him. Almost everybody in her family worked in **politics**. Maria was not sure what she wanted to do in life. She only knew she did *not* want to be in politics.

Maria boarded the campaign plane, and headed for the back. That's where the reporters sat. They got to ask all the questions, and have all the fun. Suddenly, Maria knew. She would be the one asking the questions and having the fun. She would be a TV **journalist**.

· · · · ৩৩ · · · ·

Maria Owings Shriver was born on November 6, 1955 in Chicago, Illinois. Her father, Sargent, was a **politician**. He was U. S. Ambassador to France. Her mother, Eunice, started **Special Olympics.** Eunice was a Kennedy. The Kennedys were a famous **Democratic** family.

TIDBITS

Eunice encouraged Maria to compete against the boys. Maria loved playing touch football with her brothers. "Tackle her as hard you tackle the boys!" Eunice told Sargent. "Knock her down!"

•◆•

Maria is the best-selling author of six books. Maria wrote *What's Heaven?* when NBC would not let her do a program on heaven and death. "In journalism, … you don't have a voice. You are a messenger," Maria said. Writing gave Maria her own voice.

Her uncle, John F. Kennedy, had been President of the United States. Other Kennedy uncles and cousins were senators and members of congress. Maria had a lot to live up to. She was determined to find her own way.

Eunice encouraged Maria to improve her mind. She warned Maria not to rely on her looks. She told Maria her brain would make her interesting in the long run. Maria listened, and learned.

After college, Maria worked in television news as a reporter and **news anchor**. She said, "I decided that I was going to be the Kennedy who makes her own name and finds her own job and works like a dog."

In 1977, Maria met Arnold Schwarzenegger. He was nothing like her Democratic family. He was an actor, bodybuilder, and **Republican**. The couple married in 1986. They settled in Brentwood, California and had four children.

Shortly after her wedding, Maria was fired from her news anchor job. Her TV news show was just not popular.

Maria soon found work on another news show. She started winning awards. She won an Emmy Award in 1988. She received a Christopher Award in 1990. In 1998, she earned a Peabody Award. This is one the highest honors a TV journalist can win.

Arnold ran for governor of California in 2003. Maria did not want to return to politics, but she supported her husband. When he won, California had a Republican governor and a Democratic **first lady**!

Maria planned to keep working. She loved being a TV journalist. Maria's bosses said she could not be a journalist *and* California's first lady at the same time. They thought her work would suffer. Maria had spent over 25 years building her career. Suddenly, it was gone. What would she do now?

And then Maria knew. It didn't matter *what* she did. It mattered *who* she was. Once again, Maria would find her own way. She would make her job as First Lady of California fit her. "I've tried to craft the job of First Lady in a role that reflects me. That's about connecting people, empowering, and inspiring them."

Maria has done just that. She created *It's All About WE*. The *WE* programs call on Californians to work together to build a California for working people, for poor families, for those serving in the military, for people living with disabilities — for *all* people.

First Lady, Maria Shriver announces the opening of the California Hall of Fame (2006)

Timeline: Maria Shriver

1955 ➤ November 6, Maria Owings is born the second of five children to Eunice Kennedy Shriver and Robert Sargent Shriver, Jr. She is their only daughter.

1977 ➤ June, graduates from Georgetown University with a degree in American Studies.

Works as a news writer and producer for KYW-TV in Philadelphia, Pennsylvania.

1978 ➤ Moves to WJZ-TV in Baltimore, Maryland, where she writes and produces Baltimore's *Evening Magazine* show.

1983 ➤ September, begins reporting for CBS News in New York. She is soon promoted to co-anchor of the *CBS Morning News*.

1986 ➤ April 26, marries Arnold Schwarzenegger in Hyannis, Massachusetts. They will have four children — Katherine, Christina, Patrick, and Christopher.

July, ratings for the *CBS Morning News* are low. Maria is fired.

Goes to work for NBC News.

1999 ➤ Publishes her first book, *What's Heaven?*

2003 ➤ November 17, becomes California's First Lady upon her husband's inauguration as Governor of California.

2004 ➤ Her bosses at NBC News tell Maria she must resign. They say she cannot work as a journalist while she is First Lady of California.

2008 ➤ Maria publishes her sixth book, *Just Who Will You Be? Big Question. Little Book. Answer Within.*

Learn More About Maria Shriver and Journalism

- Reeves, Diane Lindsay. *Virtual Apprentice: TV Journalist.* Checkmark Books, 2008.
- Somervill, Barbara A. *Backstage at a Newscast.* Children's Press, 2003.
- Thomas, William David. *Journalists (Cool Careers).* Gareth Stevens Publishing. 2009.

Web sites:

- The official web site of Maria Shriver, First Lady of California: http://www.firstlady.ca.gov/
- Read about the Women's Conference: http://www.californiawomen.org/
- Learn about remarkable California Women: http://www.californiamuseum.org/trails/#trails/women

Glossary

campaigned (kam PAYND) Helped someone run for political office.

Democratic (dem uh KRAT IK) One of the main political parties in the United States.

first lady (FURST LAY dee) The wife of a government leader such as a president or a governor.

journalist (JUR nuhl ist) Someone who writes for a newspaper or TV news program.

news anchor (NOOZ ANG kur) The main person who reports the news on a TV news program.

politician (pol uh TISH uhn) Someone who runs for or holds a political office such as a mayor, governor, congressman, or president.

politics (POL uh tiks) The work of running a government.

Republican (ri PUHB li kuhn) One of the main political parties in the United States.

Special Olympics (SPESH uhl oh LIM pikss) Special Olympics is an international program of year-round sports training and athletic competition for more than one million children and adults with intellectual disabilities.

Additional research conducted at:

- Miller Library and Bixler Library, Colby College, Waterville, Maine

Interview held with:

- Anita De Frantz, December 2008

Special thanks to:

- Andrea Douglas, Library Director
  Dunbarton, NH Public Library

- Lori de Leon of the Dolores Huerta Foundation

- Tip Nunn, publicist for Billie Jean King

- Lily Liu, AARP Brand Communications Manager (Historian) for her assistance
  with fact checking the profile of Ethel Percy Andrus.

- Sheila Brown, Photo Researcher

- Rukshana Singh of the Southern California Library for Social Studies and Research

A complete research bibliography for *Women of the Golden State: 25 California Women You Should Know* is available in a downloadable PDF format from Apprentice Shop Books, LLC at www.apprenticeshopbooks.com

Partial Research Bibliography *

CHAPTER 1: Juana Briones: *One of San Francisco's First Residents*

Colman, Penny. *Adventurous Women : Eight True Stories about Women Who Made a Difference.* Boston: Henry Holt & Company, 2006. 46-60.

Graham, Doug. "Barron Park History: Juana Briones Home Threatened." *Barron Park Association Newsletter. Barron Park Association Web site.* Winter 1996. Barron Park Association. 27 Oct. 2008 < http://www.bpaonline.org/www2/bp-news/1996-winter/history.html > .

Graham, Doug. "The Briones House " Legacy and Landmark." *Barron Park Association Newsletter. Barron Park Association Web site.* Spring 2005. Barron Park Association. 27 Oct. 2008 < http://www2.bpaonline.org/bp-news/2005-spring/#history > .

"Juana Briones." *Presidio of San Francisco.* National Park Service. 4 Nov. 2008 < http://www.nps.gov/prsf/historyculture/juana-briones.htm > .

CHAPTER 2: Charlotte "Charlie" Parkhurst: *Legendary Stagecoach Driver*

Bristow, Kathi. "Those Daring Stage Drivers." *California State Parks: Stagecoach Days 2008: Get On Board!* 2008. State of California. 2 Sept. 2008 < http://www.parks.ca.gov/?page_id = 25451 > .

Fradkin, Philip L. *Stagecoach: Wells Fargo and the American West.* New York: Simon & Schuster Source, 2002.

Hall, Daniel M. "The Strange Life and Times of Charley Parkhurst." *Metro Santa Cruz. News and Features.* 5-12 Mar. 2003.Metro Newspapers.2 Sept. 2008 < http://www.metroactive.com/papers/cruz/03.05.03/charley-0310.html > .

Haven, Kendall. *Amazing American Women.* Englewood, CO: Libraries Unlimited, Inc, and Its Division Teacher Ideas 1995. 242-47.

CHAPTER 3: Bridget "Biddy" Mason: *Freed Slave, Wealthy Landowner, Philanthropist*

"Biddy Mason Home Site." *A History of Black Americans in California: HISTORIC SITES.* 17 Nov. 2004. National Park Service. 29 Sept. 2008 < http://www.nps.gov/history/history/online_books/5views/5views2h14.htm > .

"Biddy Mason." 2005-2006. The African American Registry, a non-profit education organization. 25 Sept. 2008 < http://www.aaregistry.com/african_american_history/1075/from_slavery_to_entrepenur_biddy_mason___ > .

"Biddy Mason." *Women in History: Living Vignettes of Notable Women from US History.* 25 Jan. 2008. Lakewood Public Library. 25 Sept. 2008 < http://www.lkwdpl.org/wihohio/maso-bid.htm > .

Gray, Dorothy. *Women of the West.* Millbrae, CA: Les Femmes, 1976. 63-67.

Ketchum, Liza. *Into a New Country: Eight Remarkable Women of the West.* Boston: Little, Brown and Company, 2000. 40-51.

CHAPTER 4: Louise A. K. S. Clappe: *"Dame Shirley" of the Gold Rush*

Albert, Janice. "Louise A. K. S. Clappe, "Dame Shirley" (1819-1906)." *California Association of Teachers of English.* National Council of Teachers of English. 26 June 2008 < http://www.cateweb.org/CA-Author/clappe.html > .

Kurutz, Gary F. "The Shirley Letters." 26 June 2008 < http://yerbabuena1.com/shirleyetters.htm > .

Levy, JoAnn Levy. "Women in the Gold Rush." *Gold Rush.* 2004. 26 June 2008 < http://www.goldrush.com > .

CHAPTER 5: Jessie Anne Fremont: *Explorer's Wife and Writer*

Christensen, Lawrence O., William E. Foley, and Gary R. Kremer, eds. *Dictionary of Missouri Biography.* New York: University of Missouri P, 1999. 318-21.

Denton, Sally. *Passion and Principle : John and Jessie Fremont, the Couple Whose Power, Politics, and Love Shaped Nineteenth-Century America.* Grand Rapids, MI: Bloomsbury, 2007. 1-460.

Gale, Robert L. *A Cultural Encyclopedia of the 1850s in America.* Westport, CT: Greenwood P, 1993. 140-42.

"Jessie Benton Fremont." *Teacher Link.* 4 July 2008 < http://teacherlink.ed.usu.edu/tlresources/units/champions/jessiebentonfremont.pdf > .

Morrison, Dorothy N. *Under a Strong Wind : The Adventures of Jessie Benton Fremont.* New York, NY: Atheneum, 1983. 3-176.

CHAPTER 6: Alice Eastwood: *Plant Pioneer*

"Alice Eastwood Papers." *Harvard University Herbaria.* June 2002. Harvard University. 12 June 2008 < http://www.huh.harvard.edu/libraries/archives/EASTWOOD.html > .

Blakeley, Larry. "Who's in a Name: Alice Eastwood." *Who's in a Name?* 12 Nov. 2001. Cal Poly Pomona. 12 June 2008 < http://www.csupomona.edu/~larryblakely/whoname/who_east.html > .

Bonta, Marcia M., ed. *American Women Afield: Writings by Pioneering Women Naturalists.* College Station: Texas A & M UP, 1995. 84-94. This book contains two of Eastwood's letters. One describes the earthquake experience. The other is an account of a collecting trip in Portu Bodega.

Howell, John T. "Alice Eastwood, 1859 - 1953." *Taxon* 3.4 (1954): 98-100. *Academic Search Premier.* JSTOR. Miller Library, Colby College, Waterville, Maine. 26 June 2008. Keyword: Taxon.

Ogilvie, Marilyn B., and Joy D. Harvey. *Biographical Dictionary of Women of Science: Pioneering Lives From Ancient Times to the Mid-20th Century.* Vol. 1. Taylor and Francis. 395. This book is available at books.google.com.

CHAPTER 7: Maud Younger: *Millionaire Waitress*

"About Maud Younger," http://womenshistory.about.com/library/bio/blbio_younger_maud.htm

continued Partial Research Bibliography *

Clift, Eleanor. *Founding Sisters and the Nineteenth Amendment*, Hoboken, NJ: John Wiley & Sons Inc. 2003.

Hart, Vivian. *Bound By Our Constitution: Women, Workers, and the Minimum Wage,* Princeton University Press, 1994.

"Her Pressure on Congress," *New York Times*, March 2, 1919.

James, Edward T. "Maud Younger," *Notable American Women 1607-1950,* Cambridge, MA: The Belknap Press of Harvard University, 1971.

CHAPTER 8: Charlotta Bass: *Journalist and Activist*

Bass, Charlotta. *Forty Years: Memoirs from the Pages of a Newspaper*. Ms. Southern California Library for Social Studies & Research, 1960. Unpublished manuscript available from the Southern California Library for Social Studies and Research.

"Biographies: Charlotta Bass." *PBS*. 17 Sept. 2008 < http://pbs. org/blackpress/news_bios/bass.html > .

Cairns, Kathleen A. *Front-Page Women Journalists, 1920-1950*. New York: University of Nebraska P, 2003. 73-105.

Freer, Regina, and Marti Tippens. "Charlotta Bass: Her Story." *Southern California Library for Social Studies and Research*. 9 Sept. 2008 < http://www.socallib.org/bass/story/index. html > .

CHAPTER 9: Ethel Percy Andrus: *A Life of Service to Others*

"Biography: Ethel Andrus." *Ethel Andrus:Biography from Answers.com*. 19 Oct. 2008 < http://www.answers.com/ topic/ethel-andrus > .

Crippen, Dorothy. "Biography." Foreword. *Power of Years: The Wisdom of Ethel Percy Andrus*. By Dorothy Crippen, et al. Long Beach, CA: NRTA/AARP, 1968. 9-12.

CHAPTER 10: Ruth Law: *Daring Aviator*

"Girl Dies In Stunt Boarding Airplane from Running Auto." *New York Times Archives*. 5 Oct. 1921. New York Times. < http://query.nytimes.com/gst/abstract.html?res = 9d01e3 d6123eee3abc4d53dfb667838a639ede > .

Lebow, Eileen F. *Before Amelia : Women Pilots in the Early Days of Aviation*. New York: Potomac Books, Incorporated, 2002.

"Many Seek Wealth in Ruth Law's Fame." *New York Times Archives*. 24 Nov. 1916. New York Times. < http://query. nytimes.com/mem/archive-free/pdf?res = 9c06e2df153be63 3a25757c2a9679d946796d6cf > .

"Ruth Law Denies Tale She Is A Spy." *New York Times Archives*. 8 June 1918. New York Times. < http://query.nytimes. com/mem/archive-free/pdf?res = 9805efd8163ee433a2575b c0a9609c946996d6cf > .

"Ruth Law Lands Here From Chicago In Record Flight." *New York Times Archives*. 21 Nov. 1916. New York Times. < http://query.nytimes.com/mem/archive-free/pdf?res = 9b 03eedb1f3fe233a25752c2a9679d946796d6cf > .

CHAPTER 11: Dorothea Lange: *Changing the World Through Photography*

Coles, Robert (essay). *Dorothea Lange: Photographs of a Lifetime: And Aperture Monograph*, Oakland, CA: The Oakland Museum, The City of Oakland, Aperture Foundation, 1982.

"Interview with Dorothea Lange Conducted by Richard K. Doud in New York, New York, May 22, 1964," Smithsonian Archives of American Art, http://www.aaa. si.edu/collections/oralhistories/transcripts/lange64.htm

"Dorothea Lange," Films for the Humanities and Sciences.

"Dorothea Lange, Collections," Oakland Museum of California, http://www.museumca.org/global/art/collections_ dorothea_lange.html

CHAPTER 12: Mabel Fairbanks: *Skater Breaks the Ice Barrier*

Farris, Jo Ann Schneider. "Mabel Fairbanks - African American Figure Skater and Ice Skating Coach." *About.com*. < http:// figureskating.about.com/od/famousskaters/p/mabel.htm > .

Gavilanes, Nancy. "A Pioneer at the Rink is Proud of her Legacy." *New York Times* 14 Jan. 2001: 8.8.

Hopkinson, Natalie. "On Ice, Black Music and Dance Catch Fire." *The Washington Post* 19 Apr. 2003.

Jennifer, Bihm. "Pioneer Black Skater Dies." *Sentinel, Los Angeles* 17 Oct. 2001: A4.

Levine, Bettijane. "The Ice Mother Blazed the Skating Trail for Others." *Los Angeles Times* 19 Feb. 1998.

CHAPTER 13: Betty Ford: *First Lady of the United States*

"Betty Ford Biography." *Gerald R. Ford Presidential Library & Museum*. 4 Sept. 2007. 7 Dec. 2008 < www. fordlibrarymuseum.gov/grf/bbfbiop.asp > .

"Elizabeth 'Betty' Ford". *American President: An Online Reference Resource*. 2008 University of Virginia. 8 Dec. 2008 < http://millercenter.org/academic/ americanpresident/ford/essays/firstlady/elizabeth > .

"Elizabeth Bloomer Ford." *The White House*. 8 Dec. 2008 < www.whitehouse.gov/about/first_ladies/bettyford > .

"First Lady Biography: Betty Ford." *First Ladies' Biographical Information*. 2005. The National First Ladies Library. 8 Dec. 2008 < http://www.firstladies.org/biographies/ firstladies.aspx?biography = 39 > .

Greene, John Robert. *Betty Ford: Candor and Courage in the White House*. New York: University Press of Kansas, 2004.

CHAPTER 14: Tsuyako "Sox" Kitashima: *Righting the Wrongs for Japanese Americans*

Burgan, Michael. *The Japanese American Internment: Civil Liberties Denied*. New York: Compass Point Books, 2006.

"Japanese American Women and Activism Within the JA Community: Redress, Reparations, and Gender." *Discover Nikkei*. < http://www.discovernikkei.org/nikkeialbum/ en/collection/6125/item/6480 > .

* A complete research bibliography is available in downloadable PDF format from www.apprenticeshopbooks.com

continued *Partial Research Bibliography* *

"Japanese American Women and Activism Within the JA Community: Redress, Reparations, and Gender." *Discover Nikkei.* < http://www.discovernikkei.org/nikkeialbum/en/node/6125?nf = 1 > .

"Japanese Americans, A Bibliography of Children's Books." James Madison University. 16 Sept. 2008 < http://falcon.jmu.edu/ ~ ramseyil/muljapanamer.htm > .

Johnson, Jason B. "Tsuyako Kitashima 'godmother' of Japantown." *San Francisco Chronicle* 10 Jan. 2006: B-5.

CHAPTER 15: Dolores Huerta: *Activist for Migrant Workers*

De Leon, Lori. "Dolores Huerta Chapter Manuscript." Email to the author. 8 July 2008.

"Dolores Huerta." *Answers.Com.* 14 June 2008 < http://www.answes.com/topic/dolores-huerta > .

"Dolores Huerta, Biography." *Las Culturas.Com.* 2004. 6 June 2008 < http://lasculturas.com/aa/bio/bioDoloresHuerta.htm > .

"Dolores Huerta, Biography." *The Dolores Huerta Foundation.* 22 June 2008 http://dhuerta.hostcentric.com/dh_bio.htm

CHAPTER 16: Dian Fossey: *Protector of the Mountain Gorilla*

"About Dian Fossey," Dian Fossey Gorilla Fund International,www.gorillafund.org

De la Bedoyere, Camilla. *No One Loved Gorillas More: Dian Fossey Letters from the Mist,* Washington D.C.: National Geographic, 2005.

Eyden, Sally. "Lovers in the Mist: a Fascinating New TV Documentary Raises Serious

CHAPTER 17: Maxine Hong Kingston: *Writer of the Chinese American Experience*

Alegre, Miel, and Dave Weich. "Author Interviews: Maxine Hong Kingston After the Fire." *Powells.com.* 3 Dec. 2006. 17 Nov. 2008 < http://www.powells.com/authors/kingston.htm > .

Huntley, E. D. *Maxine Hong Kingston: A Critical Companion.* Westport, CT: Greenwood P, 2001.

Kingston, Maxine H. *China Men.* New York: Alfred A. Knopf, 1980.

Kingston, Maxine H. *The Women Warrior: Memoirs of a Girlhood among Ghosts.* New York: Alfred A. Knopf, 1977.

"Kingston, Maxine Hong." *1990 Current Biography Yearbook.* New York: H.W. Wilson, 1990. 259-63.

Chapter 18: Nancy Pelosi: First Woman Speaker of the House

Bzdek, Vincent. *Woman of the House: The Rise of Nancy Pelosi.* New York: Palgrave Macmillan, 2008.

"Congresswoman Nancy Pelosi: Biography." *Congresswoman Nancy Pelosi, California, 8th District.* U. S. House of Representatives. 27 Oct. 2008 < http://www.house.gov/pelosi/biography/bio.html > .

"Learn About Congress." *Kids in the House.* U.S. House of Representatives. 28 Oct. 2008 < http://clerkkids.house.gov/congress/leadership.html > .

Lewis, Peggy. "Profile: Nancy Pelosi '62 House Democratic Leader." *Trinity Washington.* Trinity University. 28 Oct. 2008 < http://www.trinitydc.edu/admissions/profiles/magazine_profile_pelosi.php > .

Pelosi, Nancy, and Amy Hill Hearth. *Know Your Power: A Message to America's Daughters.* New York: Doubleday, 2008.

CHAPTER 19: Janice Mirikitani: *Word Warrior*

Asian Women United of California, ed. *Making Waves: An Anthology of Writings by and About Asian American Women.* By Janice Mirikitani. Boston, MA: Beacon P, 1989. 349-51.

Beitiks, Edvins. "S.F.'s Poet Laureate Passes the Torch." *The Examiner* 27 Mar. 2000: A-1. *SFGate.* 27 Mar. 2000. 24 Sept. 2008 < http://www.sfgate.com/cgi-bin/article.cgi?file = /examiner/archive/2000/03/27/NEWS1859.dtl > .

Huang, Guiyou, ed. *Asian-American Poets: a Bio-Bibliographical Critical Sourcebook.* Westport, CT: Greenwood Press, 2002. 233-42. Questia Media America. 17 July 2008.

John, Crawford F., Traise Yamamoto and Maureen K. Griffin. "Janice Mirikitani." *Asian American Literature: Reviews and Criticism of Works by American Writers of Asian Descent.* Ed. Lawrence J. Trudeau. Detroit: Gale, 1998.

CHAPTER 20: Billie Jean King: *Tennis Ace and Activist*

Atkin, Ronald. "Billie Jean King." *About Wimbledon - History.* 25 July 2008 < http://aeltc2009.wimbledon.org/en_GB/about/history/billiejean_king.html > .

"Billie Jean King." *Billie Jean King: Visionary. Innovator. Champion.* 10 July 2008 < http://billiejeanking.com > .

"Billie Jean King." *I Love India: Lifestyle Lounge: Society.* 12 July 2008. 13 July 2008 < http://lifestyle.iloveindia.com/lounge/billie-jean-king-2464.html > .

"Billie Jean King." *Springfield Lasers.* 10 July 2008 < http://www.springfieldlasers.com/bjkio.htm > .

Crockett, Kathy. "Sports Hero: Billie Jean King." *My Hero.* 27 July 2008 < http://myhero.com/myhero/hero.asp?hero = bjking_06 > .

CHAPTER 21: Marcy Carsey: *TV Producer*

Alley, Robert, and Irby B. Brown. *Women Television Producers.* New York: University of Rochester P, 2001.

American Women in Radio and Television. "Marcy Carsey." *Making Waves 50 Greatest Women in Radio and Television.* Riverside, NJ: Andrews McMeel, 2001. 49-52.

Carsey, Marcy L. "Marcy Carsey." *Women's Ventures, Women's Visions: 29 Inspiring Stories from Women Who Started Their Own Business.* By Shoshana Alexander. New York: Crossing P, 1997. 84-89.

*continued Partial Research Bibliography ***

Downey, Kevin. "A Trio of Hit-Makers: Carsey, Werner Mandabach have delivered some of TV's most beloved shows (2004 Legacy Awards)." *Broadcasting & Cable* 19 Jan. 2004. *HighBeam Research.* 10 Dec. 2008 < http://www.highbeam.com/doc/1G1-112645719.html > .

CHAPTER 22: Judith Baca: *Healing with Art*

Abram, Susan, and Sue Doyle. "Iconic L.A. Murals Face Fading Future." *Inland Valley Daily Bulletin* 20 Oct. 2007. *ProQuest Newsstand.* Colby College Libraries, Waterville, ME. 20 July 2008. Keyword: L.A. murals.

Abram, Susan. "Extreme Makeover Taggers Using L.A.'s Public Murals to Showcase Their Graffiti, Ruining Years of Artists' Work." *Daily News. Los Angeles, Ca* 7 Jan. 2007, Valley ed.: n1. *ProQuest Newsstand.* Colby College Libraries, Waterville, ME.

Baca, Judith F. and Amalia M. Bains. "Oral History Interview with Judith Baca." *Smithsonian Archives of American Art.* 6 Aug. 1986. Smithsonian Institution. 1 July 2008 < http://aaa.si.edu/collections/oralhistories/transcripts/baca86.htm > .

Baca, Judith F. "A Place to Work, a Way to Tell One's Story." *Grants in the Visual Arts.* California Community Foundation. 1 July 2008 < http://www.calfund.org/arts/baca.php > .

Baca, Judith. "The Art of the Mural." *American Family.* 2004. Public Broadcasting Service. 1 July 2008 < http://www.pbs.org/americanfamily/mural.html > .

CHAPTER 23: Sally Ride: *First Woman Astronaut*

Baldwin, Louis. *Women of Strength: Biographies of 106 Who Have Excelled in Traditionally Male Fields, A.D. 61 to the Present.* Jefferson, NC: McFarland & Company, 1996. 205-07.

Felder, Deborah G. *A Century Of Women: The Most Influential Events in Twentieth-Century Women's History.* New York: Citadel P, Kensington Corp., 1999. 297-300.

Haven, Kendall, and Donna Clark. *100 Most Popular Scientists for Young Adults: Biographical Sketches and Professional Paths.* Englewood, CO: Libraries Unlimited, 1999. 406-10.

"Sally K. Ride (Ph.D.) NASA Astronaut (former)." *Lyndon B. Johnson Space Center: Biographical Data.* July 2006. National Aeronautics and Space Administration Lyndon B. Johnson Space Center. 25 Oct. 2008 < http://www.jsc.nasa.gov/Bios/htmlbios/ride-sk.html > .

"Sally Ride Biography." *Sally Ride, PhD.* 26 Jan. 2007. American Academy of Achievement. 25 Oct. 2008 < http://www.achievement.org/autodoc/page/rid0bio-1 > .

CHAPTER 24: Anita L. DeFrantz: *Olympian*

"Anita DeFrantz." *Answers.com.* 11 Dec. 2008 < http://www.answers.com/topic/anita-defrantz > .

"Anita L. DeFrantz: Bibliography." *Aetna.* Aetna Foundation. 11 Dec. 2008 < http://www.aetna.com/foundation/aahcalendar/1998defrantz_bio.html > .

"Anita Luceete DeFrantz (born 1952)." *Biographies.* University of Pennsylvania. 11 Dec. 2008 < http://www.archives.upenn.edu/people/1900s/defrantz_anita_l.html > .

CHAPTER 25: Maria Shriver: *Journalist and First Lady of California*

"California Hall of Fame." *The California Museum: Only in California.* The California Museum. < http://www.californiamuseum.org/exhibits/halloffame >

Collins, Monica. "A Problem Like Maria's." *USA Weekend* 20 Apr. 1986: 4 + .

Considine, Bob. "Maria Shriver: "I'm a Work in Progress"" *MSN.* 23 Apr. 2008. Microsoft Network. < http://www.msnbc.msn.com/id/24275209/ > .

"Dateline NBC: Checks and Balances." *Peabody Awards.* The University of Georgia. < http://www.peabody.uga.edu/winners/details.php?id = 40 > .

Maria Shriver, First Lady of California. State of California. < http://www.firstlady.ca.gov/ > .

* A complete research bibliography is available in downloadable PDF format from www.apprenticeshopbooks.com